THE JOURNAL OF THE
INSTITUTE FOR HACKS TOMFOOLERY & PRANKS
AT MIT

THE JOURNAL OF THE
INSTITUTE FOR HACKS TOMFOOLERY & PRANKS
AT MIT

Brian M. Leibowitz

The Massachusetts Institute of Technology   **THE MIT MUSEUM**   Cambridge, Massachusetts   1990

Published by
The MIT Museum
265 Massachusetts Avenue
Cambridge, Massachusetts 02139

ISBN-0-917027-03-5

Designed by David Ford

Publication of this book has been made possible in part by a grant from the
Peter De Florez '38 Fund for Humor at MIT.

Relativity © 1988 M.C. Escher Heirs / Cordon Art - Baarn - Holland
used with permission

Peanuts cartoon reprinted by permission of UFS, Inc.

"Mouth Trap" article by Bruce Sylvester
reprinted from *The Tab* with permission of the author

Excerpt reprinted from *"Surely You're Joking, Mr. Feynman!" Adventures of a Curious
Character*, Richard P. Feynman, as told to Ralph Leighton, edited by Edward Hutch-
ings, by permission W.W. Norton and Company, Inc.
Copyright © 1985 by Richard P. Feynman and Ralph Leighton

10 9 8 7 6 5 4 3 2

To everyone who made this publication possible—
if I don't know who you are, you do.

CONTENTS

FOREWORD

In 1959, while in the Air Force and stationed in Boston, I was on an investigative team looking into telephone usage by certain MIT students. By systematically deciphering dialing codes, these students had infiltrated the highest levels of Defense Department communications. During this inquiry I learned that pranks—far more ingenious and whimsical than interrupting telecommunications—were a time-honored MIT tradition.

Throughout the 1970s, when the Museum canvassed the MIT community for historic materials, a wealth of prank-related photos was unearthed. Written references to pranks and other inexplicable goings-on, some dating back to the Institute's earliest days, also came to light. This file of prank-related materials soon became the Museum's most researched collection, and articles on specific pranks garnered international attention.

An in-depth study of pranks (in MITese, "hacks") began in the early 1980s when grad student Bob Baldwin '79 produced a slide lecture drawn from our files and other sources. A publication was discussed at that time, but, as sometimes happens to grad students, Bob got his PhD and joined the corporate world in sunny CA. Providentially, another hacker extraordinaire, grad student Brian Leibowitz '82, assumed the mantle of the Museum's curator of the Institute for Hacks, TomFoolery, and Pranks at MIT. Brian's work on this much anticipated volume has been a labor of blood, sweat, and laughs, resulting in the ultimate satisfaction that only such an endeavor can offer.

Enjoy!

Warren A. Seamans 'HM
DIRECTOR, THE MIT MUSEUM

NEXTWORD

Let's face it. MIT has a reputation as a serious place, a think tank, a paradigm of intellect, imagination, and ingenuity. While this may be true, there is another aspect of the Institute little known to the world beyond: MIT's long-standing tradition of humor.

And I am not, most emphatically, referring to techno-wizards chuckling over cold fusion or swapping jokes with mathematical equations in the punch line. I'm talking about pranks—high-tech hi-jinks. Over the past century or so the MIT prank has developed into today's permutation—The Hack.

The spirit of MIT, its inventiveness and thoroughness, finds expression in the lighthearted project as well as the scholarly. Humor at MIT might be considered an anomaly by some, but is, in fact, the warp of the fabric of this unique community. As you read through *The Journal of the Institute for Hacks, TomFoolery, and Pranks at MIT* you will see that even the president of this august institution is not immune from the hacker's thrust.

Paul E. Gray '54
PRESIDENT, MIT

GLOSSARY

APO Alpha Phi Omega, national service fraternity.

ATO Alpha Tau Omega, fraternity.

Baker House Dormitory.

Beast from the East Second East, East Campus dormitory.

Beaver MIT mascot.

Brass Rat The MIT class ring. Named for the beaver on the face of the ring.

Burton House Dormitory.

DKE Delta Kappa Epsilon, fraternity.

East Campus Dormitory.

FDC Freshman Defense Corps. A group that provided water weapons to freshmen before the traditional freshman shower night in the early 1980s.

Great Dome The larger of two domes crowning the main buildings at MIT.

Hack n.   A prank, usually elaborate.   v.   1) To perform a prank. 2) To explore the places on campus that are not usually accessible. 3) To work at or study a subject not especially for academic gain.

Hacker One who hacks.

Harvard The red brick school up the creek from MIT.

Harvard Bridge The bridge over the Charles River near MIT. (see Smoot)

Hell MIT.

I.H.T.F.P. MIT acronym with many meanings: Institute Has The Finest Professors, I Have Taken Freshman Physics, I Have Truly Found Paradise, It's Hard To Fondle Penguins, and I Hate This Place.

Jack E. Florey Imaginary resident of Fifth East, East Campus.

James E. Tetazoo Imaginary resident of Third East, East Campus.

Killian Court (also known as the Great Court) Large courtyard surrounded on three sides by the older campus buildings and open towards the Charles River on the fourth.

Lobby 7 The lobby under the small dome, the main entrance to MIT.

MacGregor House Dormitory.

Nerd (also nurd or gnurd) One who studies too much, especially a tiresome, socially ineffective overachiever.

ORK Order of Random Knights (from the Random Hall dormitory).

R/O Residence and Orientation week.

Rush n. 1) The time when new members are recruited to join living groups. At MIT, dormitories, fraternities, and independent living groups have rush during R/O. 2) Common with the freshmen and sophomores around the turn of the century, a rush was a scrimmage between two groups of students. v. To recruit new members to a living group.

Senior House Dormitory.

Small Dome Above Lobby 7, the smaller of two domes crowning the main buildings at MIT.

Smoot Unit of length used to measure the Harvard Bridge—approximately 5'6". The bridge is 364.4 Smoots plus 1 ear.

The Tech Student newspaper published since 1881.

Tech Talk Administration newspaper published by the MIT News Office since 1957.

Technique MIT yearbook.

Technology Review Science and technology magazine published by the MIT Alumni Association since 1899. Originally chronicling developments at MIT and the writings of the MIT community, Technology Review has expanded into an internationally respected science publication dealing with the impact of science and technology on society.

THA Technology Hackers Association.

Tool v. To study. n. A person who studies all the time.

Voo Doo Student humor magazine originated in 1919.

THE JOURNAL OF THE
INSTITUTE
FOR HACKS
TOMFOOLERY
& PRANKS
AT MIT

INTRODUCTION

In his memoirs, noted civil engineer John Ripley Freeman, class of 1876, recalled "episodes when iodide of nitrogen [a mild contact explosive] was sprinklered [sic] on the drill room floor just before the assembly." This is the earliest documented student prank at MIT. Articles in an anonymous column, "The Lounger," in the student newspaper, *The Tech,* indicate that MIT students in the late nineteenth century pulled many pranks—the details of which are unfortunately sparse.

Student pranks at MIT have come to be known as *hacks.* A hack differs from the ordinary college prank in that the event usually requires careful planning, engineering, and finesse and has an underlying wit and inventiveness. The unwritten rule holds that a hack should be good-natured, non-destructive, and safe. In fact, hackers sometimes assist in dismantling their handiwork.

In the late nineteenth century and the first half of the twentieth, the inventiveness and wit associated with hacks was also seen in the rivalry between the classes. Prior to the annual freshman-sophomore football game, each class would attempt to raise its class flag on the flagpole and try to prevent the other class from removing it. This often involved climbing the pole to secure the flag and then greasing or barricading the pole to prevent the opposing class from raising its flag. Each year, the defensive methods grew more elaborate.

Following the football game, freshmen and sophomores competed in the Cane Rush, a melee for possession of a four-foot stick with a knob on each end; the winner was the team with the most hands on the stick after fifteen minutes. This event ended tragically in 1900 with the death of a freshman and the Cane Rush was immediately discontinued.

Class competition continued the next year with the inception of Field Day, consisting of the traditional football game, a tug-of-war, and a relay race. In 1927, the Glove Fight was added. In this event, freshmen wore white gloves on their left hands and sophomores wore red gloves on their right hands. The object was to capture as many of the other team's gloves as possible and place them in a barrel. A defensive tactic was to hide the glove in one's clothing. A counter strategy quickly evolved, however, to put all of an opponent's clothes in the barrel and assume that the glove would be among them.

Class rivalry escalated in the weeks before Field Day. Many inter-class hacks were performed and many traditions developed. Sophomores would rearrange the furniture in the freshmen's rooms or initiate epic-scale waterfights when freshmen returned from class meetings. Both classes would hang banners in inaccessible public places and the rival class would feel compelled to remove them.

In the late fifties, the intense class rivalry surrounding Field Day faded. To meet the changing interests of students, Field Day was modified to include events requiring ingenuity and organization as well as athletic skill. The fifties also saw the beginnings of the MIT term *hack*. The origin of the term in the MIT slang is elusive—different meanings have come in and out of use and it was rarely used in print before the 1970s. Furthermore, the use of *hack* varied among different groups of students at MIT. *Hacking* was used by many MIT students to describe any activity undertaken to avoid studying—this could include "goofing off," playing bridge, talking to friends, or going out. Performing pranks was also called *hacking*, but only as part of the broader definition. In the middle to late fifties, additional meanings for the word *hack* were developed by members of the Tech Model Railroad Club, including an article or project without constructive end or an unusual and original solution to a problem such as inventing a new circuit for a switching system. In the late fifties, students on campus began to use the word as a noun to describe a prank.

Also in the late fifties, *telephone hacking,* the study of the internal codes and features of telephone switching systems, emerged. Here, the word *hack* was used to imply doing something outside the norm; telephone systems were made to do things that the system designers never anticipated.

Concurrent with the growth of student activism in the sixties, enthusiasm for Field Day waned and the event was eliminated in 1968. The sixties also saw class rivalry give way to living-group loyalty. In the seventies, Field Day reemerged as Spring Weekend, with parties and inter-living-group competitions.

This shift of loyalty from the class to the living group changed the character of hacking at MIT; as less time was devoted to class rivalries and class events, more time was devoted to other activities, including hacking. The scope of hacking also expanded—hacks directed at the MIT community became more common.

In the late sixties and the seventies, the meaning of the word *hack* broadened to include activities that tested limits of skill, imagination, and wits. *Hacking* was investigating a subject for its own sake and not for academic advancement, exploring the normally inaccessible places on campus, doing something clandestine or out of the ordinary, and performing pranks.

The word *hack* found its way into common usage outside MIT with the advent of *computer hacking* in the early sixties. In the eighties, experts in the computer field made a distinction between *hacking* and *cracking*. Hacking denotes nondestructive mischief while *cracking* describes activities such as unleashing a computer virus, breaking into a computer, or destroying data.

By the mid-eighties, *hacking* had come to be used at MIT primarily to describe pranks and exploring the Institute. Many of the earlier definitions have disappeared from use on campus.

Hacks are not performed by any one kind of MIT student. Many hacks are perpetrated by living groups, student organizations, informal organizations formed specifically for hacking or by small groups of individuals. The reasons for hacking at MIT are as diverse as the students. Every student or group that hacks is unique with different interests and motivations. Each hack is an individual event inspired by different circumstances and situations.

The hacks described in this book are verified and documented with photos, newspaper articles, or first-person accounts. Owing to the clandestine nature of hacks, the quality of photographs and the depth of description vary among the hacks depicted. Wherever known, the group responsible is identified. Except when reprinted in a newspaper article, no individual names are given in deference to those hackers who might wish to remain anonymous.

I am the merry wanderer of the night.
I jest to Oberon, and make him smile.

A Midsummer Night's Dream

BUILDINGS

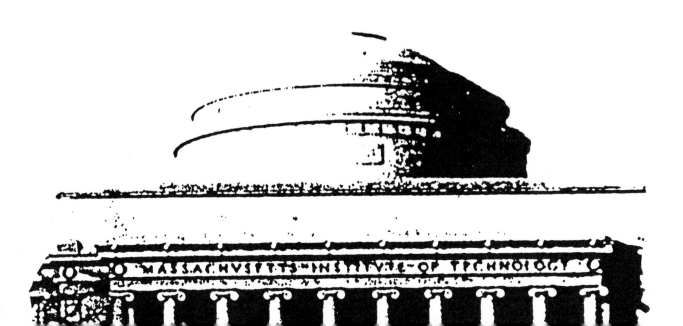

To the world at large, MIT's two massive domes are the signature of its campus. To the MIT hacker, however, they are two imposing canvases demanding adornment. The small dome is 100 feet high, and stretches 72 feet across the main entrance at 77 Massachusetts Avenue. The great dome, which tops the Barker Engineering Library, is 150 feet high and 108 feet across. Both were patterned after the ancient Roman Pantheon.

BUILDINGS

7

Grayer Pastures

A life-size fiberglass steer "borrowed" from the Hilltop Steak House in Saugus, Massachusetts found its way to the top of the great dome. When "Ferdi" returned home, the Hilltop's management placed a mortar board on its head and a diploma in its mouth.

ATO / OCTOBER 31, 1979

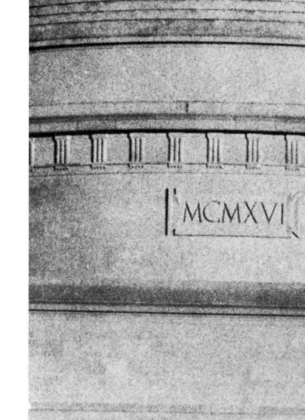

Kilroy Was Here

Peering out over Massachusetts Avenue, George was created one Halloween night with six thousand square feet of polyethylene sheeting and a few flourishes of paint. George was removed early the next morning, however, and few people saw him.

A letter to *The Tech* asked, "... what harm would there have been to let poor George exist for one full day? The spirit of the Institute dies again as the bureaucracy acted efficiently only in destroying something that only could've brought a smile and chuckle to the people who normally trudge in and out of the 77 Massachusetts Ave. entrance.... In any event, for no matter how short a time it was ... Kilroy was here."

A few nights later, George reappeared and was allowed to remain for a full day.

MACGREGOR DORMITORY / OCTOBER 31, 1972 AND NOVEMBER 6, 1972

Returning the Favor

A giant wood screw is a reoccurring image at MIT. It is the symbol and trophy for the annual "Institute Screw" award, a charity contest held by APO each year when the MIT community chooses the individual who has done the best job of "screwing" the students. The Big Screw is depicted embedded in the great dome on the popular IHTFP T-shirt. Both the small dome and the great dome have been adorned with screws.

ATO / OCTOBER 31, 1977

MECHANICAL ENGINEERING STUDENTS / MAY 1985

Home on the Dome

To help alleviate crowding in the dormitories, Room 10-1000 was added to the great dome. Sixteen feet square and twelve feet high, blue with windows and a door painted on, 10-1000 was complete with mailbox and welcome mat. The twenty-eight panels of the room were hauled up the side of the building, then assembled with hinges on the inside, which made the room difficult to dismantle. The structure was then secured with cables and ropes. Owing to intervention by the campus police, the roof was never installed.

THA / SEPTEMBER 1986

A Summer Snowman

On a hot summer day in 1987, a 5' 7" papier-mâché "snowperson" appeared on the small dome.

THA / AUGUST 1987

PEANUTS ®   By Charles M. Schulz

Reprinted by permission of UFS, Inc.

It's the Great Pumpkin, Charlie Brown

The most haunting hack on the great dome was inspired by Linus Van Pelt from Charles Schulz' comic strip *Peanuts*. According to the cartoon, Linus spends every Halloween night in the pumpkin patch waiting for the Great Pumpkin. Said an ATO spokesman, "It seemed a humanitarian thing to do—to make the 'Great Pumpkin' rise out of the pumpkin patch on Halloween so that the Linuses of the world would not be disillusioned."

The nose and mouth of the Great Pumpkin were painted on a piece of cloth that was hung on the side of the dome, the eyes fashioned with water-soluble paint, and the orange tint created by placing red and yellow filters in front of the floodlights that illuminated the dome.

OCTOBER 31, 1962

The Great Breast of Knowledge

The notion that the great dome resembles a giant breast was first suggested in the living group Burton One in December 1978. During IAP (Independent Activities Period) in January 1979, blueprints of the dome were studied and the proper dimensions for the nipple and aureole were determined. The nipple was then constructed using a wooden frame covered with chicken wire and pink paper.

As hackers prepared to haul it up the side of the building, campus police came upon the nipple sitting on the roof of the car. Undaunted by this setback, the group planned their second attempt. This time practice sessions were held to hone climbing skills and to reduce the time needed to transfer the nipple from the car to the roof. Alas, preparations notwithstanding, implementation was foiled again—the hackers were spotted by a cleaning woman, so they decided once again to postpone the hack.

Alleged treachery barred the Burton group's third attempt, when campus police, acting on an anonymous tip, arrived at the scene to stop what they had been led to believe was a robbery in progress. Their escape hampered by a snagged rope, two members of the hacker roof crew were caught. After a chat with the campus police chief, the students agreed not to try again that semester. Later learning that the anonymous tipster may have been a student from another floor of their own dorm, the hackers realized that secrecy was now essential to their success.

The annual freshman picnic marked the beginning of a new semester and a new plan was formed. A redesigned, collapsible nipple did not have to be brought up the side of the building, but could be carried in backpacks. On this, their fourth attempt, the Burton hackers announced to their dormitory that the project had been called off. Finally, during the freshman picnic, the Burton One Outdoor Breast Society successfully installed the Great Breast of Knowledge with its accompanying banner: "Mamma Maxima Scientiae."

BURTON ONE OUTDOOR BREAST SOCIETY / AUGUST 1979

"It's for you"

When the campus police discovered a telephone booth with working lights on the great dome, the phone immediately started ringing. An officer radioed to headquarters, "The phone's ringing; what should I do?" The reply, "Well, why don't you answer it?"

Happy 100th MIT

Members of the freshman class celebrated MIT's centennial with a nine-foot-tall cardboard candle on the great dome and a banner reading, "Happy Birthday."

CLASS OF 1964 / APRIL 1961

Miss Liberty Comes to Cambridge

On July 4, 1986, the Boston Pops went to New York for the rededication of the Statue of Liberty and could not play their traditional concert on the Boston Esplanade. The hackers decided that trading the Pops for the Statue was fair and resolved to bring Miss Liberty to Cambridge.

Preparations were undertaken quickly, as the hack was conceived only five days before the Fourth. The crown was constructed using triangular sleeves of white cloth mounted on aluminum masts. Each mast stood atop a wooden base with carpeting underneath to prevent scratching the dome. Guy wires kept the crown in position. Liberty's flaming torch was fashioned with a simple yellow sheet attached to the crow's nest beside the dome.

Implementation of the hack was initially snagged when the hackers discovered that an extension ladder needed to reach the hatch on the dome would fit in neither the elevator nor the stairs. The key to a successful hack, however, is foresight and ingenuity and in this instance, the hackers had brought a 300-foot length of rope. With much effort, the ladder was hauled up the side of the building. A hacker wearing a safety harness then mounted the dome, guided the string of spikes around the lightning rod, and made the final adjustments.

THE EVEN EXCHANGE COMMISSION / JULY 4, 1986

Happy Radome

The Cecil and Ida Green Building is 277 feet tall with a 26.5-foot-diameter radar dome on the roof. Faces on the sides of the radar dome appeared one night looking out on both Cambridge and Boston.

The happy faces were painted on yellow building tarps tied together into a cylinder and deployed through a hatch on the top of the radar dome. Drawstrings on the top and bottom held the tarps against the dome. The tarps were borrowed from a building under construction and were later returned.

THA / FEBRUARY 1983

Greenspeak

1, 2) Greenspeak was first employed in March 1964 (before the Green Building was completed) by Theta Chi (ΘX) fraternity. The next night, "Jack Florey" decided to use the same medium to advertise its feelings about MIT.

3) In October 1985, the Fred Underground Hackers used Greenspeak to advertise a proposal to rename the East Campus dormitory "Fred."

4) In July 1969, the Apollo 11 mission brought Neil Armstrong and Edwin "Buzz" Aldrin Jr., '63 to the surface of the moon. The Green Building celebrated the historic event.

5, 6) When the Boston Red Sox played the 1986 World Series, the Prudential Tower in Boston was lighted with a giant "1." The "Group On the Study Of Xenoliths" used the Green Building, located across the river from the "Pru," to display "SOX," that is, after overcoming the resistance of a loyal Mets fan who refused to close his shade. After the Mets won the series, other hackers created a large "2" on the Green Building.

7) Greenspeak was used to direct freshmen to the East Campus dormitory during R/O 1979.

8, 9) The Green Building was decorated appropriately for Christmas in 1973 and for Halloween in 1975.

1

2

3

4

5

6

7

8

9

Piling It Higher and Deeper

The Green Building was not immune from hackers even during construction. This "Tech is Hell" banner appeared on the pile driver.

JANUARY 1962

Kilroy Was Here

A sign was taped to the windowless side of the Green Building approximately seventeen stories off the ground.

Mint Green

The black, red, and yellow squares decorating the tiled exterior of the Wiesner Arts and Media Building are part of a collaboration between the architects, I. M. Pei & Partners, and an artist, Kenneth Noland. The fourth colored square, mint green, was not part of the original design. The green square was taken off a few days prior to the dedication ceremony. It promptly reappeared, but was removed again the morning of the dedication.

JAMES E. TETAZOO / MARCH 1985

Don't Rain on My Dedication

During the dedication ceremony for the Wiesner Building, five pounds of colored confetti, 180 two-inch strips of magnetic computer tape, and 175 fish-shaped paper airplanes spewed from ventilation ducts in the atrium. To add to the success of the hack, Paul Gray '54, president of MIT, happened to be standing directly under the ducts when the confetti fell.

OCTOBER 1985

Double Word Score

The grid of white tiles on the exterior of the Wiesner Building inspired
a crossword advertisement during freshman orientation week.

BEAST FROM THE EAST / AUGUST 1986

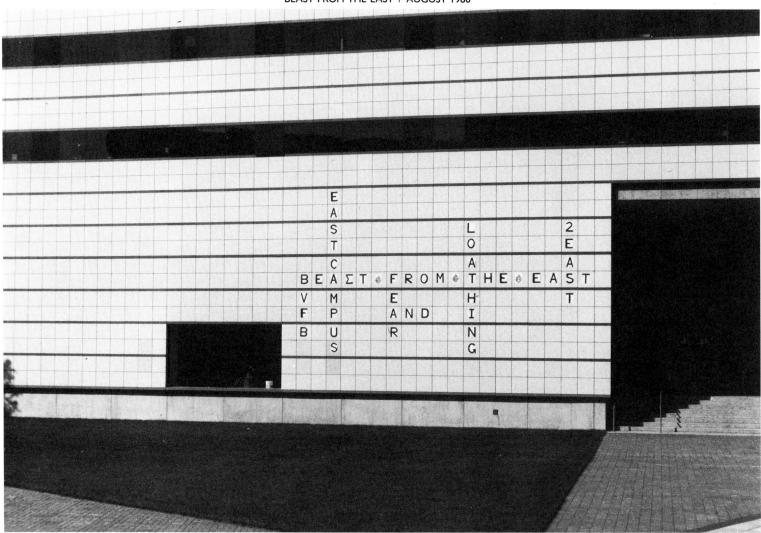

Tire Swing on the Arts and Media Building

JACK E. FLOREY / C. 1986

Indoor Sailing

In 1960, students decided to go sailing on the Alumni Swimming Pool in a Tech Dinghy.

Twenty-seven years later student sailors took to the pool again.

NOVEMBER 1960

JANUARY 1987

Jackson Sux

Students moving into the new MacGregor Dormitory in September 1970 found plumbing and electrical problems and many areas of the building unfinished. An additional cornerstone was added to the building in November expressing the students' feelings about the contractor of the building.

MACGREGOR DORMITORY / NOVEMBER 1970

Massachusetts Toolpike

The seemingly endless hallway that runs from the 77 Massachusetts Avenue entrance in Lobby 7 for 775 feet straight through to the far reaches of Building 8 is known, fittingly, as the Infinite Corridor.

The Massachusetts Toolpike (*Tool* is an MIT expression for studying) was created by laying a double line of yellow tape down the length of the Infinite Corridor dividing it into lanes. Exit signs, toll advisories, traffic regulation signs, a rotary, and turn lanes were added and, of course, a car was parked in the lobby of Building 10.

THA / 1985

Parking at the Walker Memorial Building

1930

1959

Stoplight

Painted red, yellow, and green by hackers, the three round windows in the atrium of the Health Services Center directed pedestrian traffic one fall afternoon.

BIZZARRO / SEPTEMBER 1988

Statuesque Student

Four vacant pedestals have stood in the corners of Lobby 7 since the building was completed in 1938. For a few hours in the spring of 1979 a student served as a living monument on one of these pedestals.

APRIL 1979

Ping-Pong Balls from on High

To perk up a winter day in 1983, sixteen hundred pink and green Ping-Pong balls were dropped by remote control from the 90-foot domed ceiling of Lobby 7. Falling at a rate of approximately ten per second, it took more than two and a half minutes for the balls to drop.

THA / JANUARY 1983

Random Die

This space station structure was erected by graduate students in the Department of Architecture's Building Technology Group. The five-meter-wide cube of aluminum tubing was a prototype frame designed to hold modules in the planned US space station. ORK decided to use the frame to create the world's largest die.

First, a two-foot scale model was built and hung with ropes in the same arrangement as the original. Next, a procedure was developed for wrapping the 1600 square feet of cloth around the cube. This was especially difficult because flaps of cloth had to be fitted together and tied while the structure was thirty feet in the air. As is usual in an endeavor of this nature, logistical problems arose and additional guy ropes and "sky hooks" were necessary to position and secure the covering.

Two signs were attached to the die. One announced a lecture on "The Study of Random Numbers Through the Use of First Order Procedure Objects." The announced time and place corresponded with a real lecture in a Computer Science course on "First Order Procedure Object." The second sign warned against hanging objects from the structure.

PROCEDURE

Ropes 1-4 come down
2 thrown over A
1 thrown over B
3 thrown over A
4 thrown over B

Ropes 5-8 come down
5 thrown over B
6 thrown over A
7 thrown over A

Cloth lowered halfway
Pull 4,5,6,7,8 to spread cloth
Cloth lowered to top of cube

2+3 pulled over corner towards C

2+3 thrown over C
Rope trick with 1+2
Ladder set up under cube
Pull 1 to bottom corner
Pull 3 to bottom corner
People in Dome leave with rope 9

4 thrown over C
6 thrown over C

All ropes to bottom corner
Tie 3, 1, 4, and 6 to cube
Pull 5, 7, and 9 to bottom
Ladder Man secures grommets w/cable
Everyone leaves area

Cable B

Cable A

Cable C

corridor

Top View

ORK / SEPTEMBER 1986

Quasquicentennial Banner

When MIT celebrated its 125th anniversary, "Jack Florey" decided to honor the hacking tradition with a banner hung inside the small dome. A note left inside the ceiling instructed physical plant workers that the banner was authorized by the dean's office and to contact the dean for student affairs before removing it. The dean, of course, knew nothing about it.

JACK E. FLOREY / 1986

SIGNS

Salmonella de Puerto Rico Café

A dining hall was closed during renovations of the student center in the 1987-1988 school year; a temporary dining hall was set up in the Sala de Puerto Rico named "Starvin' Marvin's Café." A large sign was placed outside the student center displaying the new name.

One night, the sign changed. . . .

THA / NOVEMBER 1987

Escher Designs the Student Center

An exhibit at the Julius A. Stratton Student Center contained the architect's drawings and floor plans for the renovation of the building. The staircase in one of the drawings reminded some students of M. C. Escher's impossible buildings. An Escher print was placed over the original rendering.

SUMMER 1988

More Signs

The Tech - June 3, 1925

Dorms Transformed Into Suffolk Co. Jail

Exactly on time, in accordance with placards that had been placed around the dormitories, an electric sign, heralded by loud reports, proclaimed to the world that '93 Dormitory had been changed into the Suffolk County Jail. Notices had been spread about, telling the inhabitants of the old dorms "to watch '93 at 11.30."

At half past eleven several autos drove up to the new dormitories and ten or a dozen men piled out, carrying something heavy. Scarcely had they gotten in the door when a loud explosion took place, all lights in the corridors and stairways flickered and went out, and all eyes were strained to see what was about to happen. In a few moments the onlookers were rewarded. A big electric sign bearing the words "Suffolk County Jail" flamed out in the darkness. After a short exhibition, the sign was spirited away, and, according to latest reports, had not been located.

EARLY 1970S

1977

1987

C. 1987

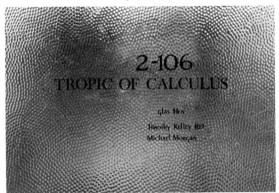

2-106
TROPIC OF CALCULUS

glas Hen

Timothy Kelley RD
Michael Morgan

1985

M.I.T. monster
EaTs
Boston / Back Bay

1969

FRESHMAN
ADVISORY
COUNCIL

Advise
5t)

1971

DEPARTMENT OF
HEAVEN
AND
EARTH

MAY 1960

1970S

1987

Center for Theatrical Physics

1971

TWENTY CHIM
WESTERN STRIP STEAK   150
HALF LB CHOPPED BEEFSTEAK 100
WIESNER NITZEL   125
BOSTON SOLE   90
BARBEQUED CHICKEN   100
FRIED CHICKEN   100
FISH SANDWICH   50
ABOVE ITEMS A LA CARTE
                   SANDWICHES
AST BEEF   85   CORN

PRE 1960

4-273
DEPARTMENT
OF
ALCHEMY

W.

EARLY 1980'S

DEPARTMENT of ALCHEMY

FEBRUARY 1984

C. 1970

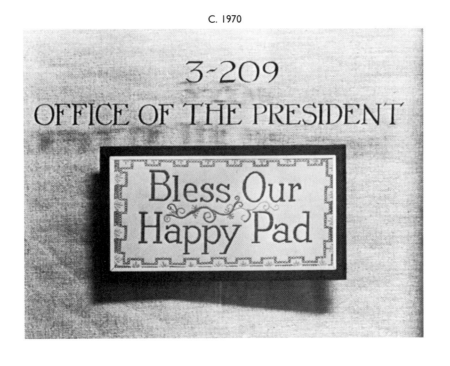

3-209
OFFICE OF THE PRESIDENT

Bless Our
Happy Pad

1980'S

SHERATON

The brothers of Alpha Tau Omega succeeded in changing the sign on the Sheraton Boston hotel to advertise their fraternity during R/O. A switch, discovered on the night of the hack, turned off the first four letters, reducing the necessary work. The "N" was blocked off by a frame covered with plastic and black oilcloth. Since then, the Sheraton has graciously advertised ATO for one night each year during R/O.

No Flaming

The city of Cambridge passed an ordinance prohibiting smoking in the workplace. "SMOKING PROHIBITED BY LAW" signs were posted throughout the Institute. An announcement of the policy was distributed to the MIT community. Soon after, "FLAMING PROHIBITED BY LAW" signs appeared around the Institute and a flier parodying the official announcement was distributed around campus. Flaming is defined in the 1989 edition of *HowToGAMIT* as "speaking obnoxiously and/or at great length."

APRIL 1987

THE FRESHMAN PICNIC

Residence and orientation period (known as R/O) includes the freshman picnic. The freshmen are greeted by the MIT president, the director of admissions, student government officers, the dean for student affairs, and other notables. Hackers greet freshmen in their own way:

The first freshman picnic hack was a 1975 banner by "James Tetazoo": "ABANDON ALL HOPE YE WHO ENTER HERE." The quote is from the inscription on the gates of Hell in Dante's *The Inferno*.

JAMES E. TETAZOO / 1975

JAMES E. TETAZOO / 1977

In 1977, the same group confused freshmen with a different greeting. . .

. . . and in 1979 with a line from Edgar Allan Poe's "The Cask of Amontillado." These are the last words spoken by a man as the last brick is placed sealing him into a wall forever.

UPPER BANNER: JAMES E. TETAZOO / LOWER BANNER: ORK / 1979

Since 1979, many different groups have displayed banners.

UPPER BANNER: FDC / LOWER BANNER: THA / 1981

FRESHMAN PICNIC

FRESHMAN PICNIC

FRESHMAN PICNIC

Phantom of Kresge

In 1986 the welcoming speeches to the freshmen were given in Kresge Auditorium. During the MIT president's speech, the pipe organ mysteriously began playing Bach's "Toccata and Fugue in D Minor" without a visible organist.

Everybody loves a good hack.

FRESHMAN PICNIC

LIVING GROUPS

Doors

At many schools, the practice of "pennying" a door shut is common. At MIT more creative methods are used.

C. 1973

C. 1937

1984

C. 1984

C. 1946

C. 1973

MIT students have often found the doors to their rooms missing. One of Tech's more famous alumni, Richard P. Feynman '39 (recipient of countless honors, including the 1965 Nobel Prize for Physics), described a door incident in his autobiography, *"Surely You're Joking, Mr. Feynman!"*:

My masterpiece of mischief happened at the fraternity [Phi Beta Delta]. One morning I woke up very early, about five o'clock, and couldn't go back to sleep, so I went downstairs from the sleeping rooms and discovered some signs hanging on strings which said things like "DOOR! DOOR! WHO STOLE THE DOOR?" I saw that someone had taken a door off its hinges, and in its place they hung a sign that said, "PLEASE CLOSE THE DOOR!"—the sign that used to be on the door that was missing.

I immediately figured out what the idea was. In that room a guy named Pete . . . and a couple of other guys liked to work very hard, and always wanted it quiet. If you wandered into their room looking for something, or to ask them how they did problem such and such, when you would leave you would always hear these guys scream, "Please close the door!"

Somebody had gotten tired of this, no doubt, and had taken the door off. Now this room, it so happened, had two doors, the way it was built, so I got an idea: I took the other door off its hinges, carried it downstairs, and hid it in the basement behind the oil tank. Then I quietly went back upstairs and went to bed.

Later in the morning I made believe I woke up and came downstairs a little late. The other guys were milling around, and Pete and his friends were all upset: The doors to their room were missing, and they had to study, blah, blah, blah, blah. I was coming down the stairs and they said, "Feynman! Did you take the doors?"

"Oh, yeah!" I said. "*I* took the door. You can see the scratches on my knuckles here, that I got when my hands scraped against the wall as I was carrying it down into the basement."

They weren't satisfied with my answer; in fact, they didn't believe me.

The guys who took the first door had left so many clues—the handwriting on the signs, for instance—that they were soon found out. . . .

The other door stayed missing for a whole week, and it became more and more important to the guys who were trying to study in that room that the other door be found.

Finally, in order to solve the problem, the president of the fraternity says at the dinner table, "We have to solve this problem of the other door. I haven't been able to solve the problem myself, so I would like suggestions from the rest of you as to how to straighten this out, because Pete and the others are trying to study."

Somebody makes a suggestion, then someone else.

After a little while, I get up and make a suggestion. "All right," I say in a sarcastic voice, "whoever you are who stole the door, we know you're wonderful. You're so *clever!* We can't figure out *who* you are, so you must be some sort of supergenius. You don't have to tell us who you are; all we want to know is where the door is. So if you will leave a note somewhere, telling us where the door is, we will honor you and admit *forever* that you are a super-marvel, that you are so *smart* that you could take the other door without our being able to figure out who you are. But for God's sake, just leave the note somewhere, and we will be forever grateful to you for it."

The next guy makes his suggestion: "I have another idea," he says. "I think that you, as president, should ask each man on his word of honor towards the fraternity to say whether he took the door or not."

The president says, "That's a *very* good idea. On the fraternity word of honor!" So he goes around the table, and asks each guy, one by one: "Jack, did *you* take the door?"

"No, sir, I did not take the door."

"Tim: Did *you* take the door?"

"No, sir! I did not take the door."

"Maurice. Did *you* take the door?"

"No, I did not take the door, sir."

"Feynman, did *you* take the door?"

"Yeah, *I* took the door."

"Cut it out, Feynman; this is *serious*! Sam! Did *you* take the door . . ."—it went all the way around. Everyone was *shocked*. There must be some real *rat* in the fraternity who didn't respect the fraternity word of honor!

That night I left a note with a little picture of the oil tank and the door next to it, and the next day they found the door and put it back.

Sometime later I finally admitted to taking the other door, and I was accused by everybody of lying. They couldn't remember what I had said. All they could remember was their conclusion after the president of the fraternity had gone around the table and asked everybody, that nobody admitted taking the door. The idea they remembered, but not the words.

People often think I'm a faker, but I'm usually honest, in a certain way—in such a way that often nobody believes me!

Richard Feynman's antics did not stop when he left MIT. Throughout his life he was well known as a practical joker.

The Tech - February 2, 1925

Lost Door Mystery Is Laid to Dorm Goblin

Mystery surrounds the latest exploit of the dormitory ghost. Friday evening one of the men living in the Class of '93 dormitory returned from dinner to find his room door missing. Alarmed at this new turn the long dormant spirit had taken, the victim brought the dormitory watchman to the scene. Aided by a member of the Cambridge Police Department, the searchers found the door under the mattress on the bed. No trace has been found of the goblin.

This is the first manifestation that the dorm men have had that the spectre is still abroad. Last fall it was active, but so far this year it has kept under cover.

Congested Rooms

C. 1973

C. 1936

C. 1963

C. 1942

1940

C. 1984

1963

C. 1936

C. 1943

LIVING GROUPS

63

Railroaded

Reprinted from a newspaper article—source unknown - c. 1936.

TECH BOYS' ROOM LAID WITH RAILS
TRACKS WELDED ELECTRICALLY TO GREET STUDENTS ON RETURN

The ingenuity of budding young M.I.T. engineers took the form of a welcome to two Bronxville, N.Y. seniors who will return from a weekend at their homes early today.

In their room at the D. K. E. fraternity house ... [they] will find two steel railroad tracks snugly fitted diagonally across the chamber—and electrically welded.

In recent years, Tech pranksters have engineered an automobile into another of the rooms of the Deke House, and once hoisted an ancient car to the roof of a dormitory. While the problem of removing the welded rails might puzzle laymen, the solution is simple to M.I.T. genius. Just "unweld" them.

Well Wishers

A freshman, returning from a tour with the MIT Concert Band, found a sign on his door, "Best Wishes, The Hall." When he opened his door, he was showered with pennies and found a wishing well in the center of his room. The structure required more than one hundred man-hours, approximately two hundred bricks, and was furnished complete with a sandy bottom, a foot of water, and a scattering of pennies.

JAMES E. TETAZOO / FEBRUARY 1973

One Room, River View

A set of dorm room furniture was moved to the middle of the frozen Charles River.

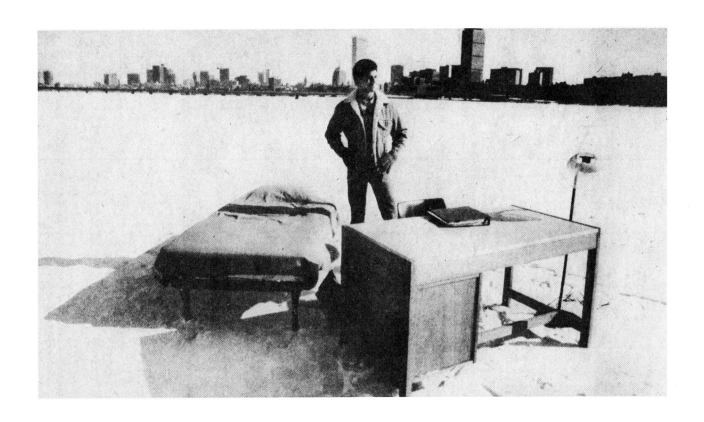

BURTON / FEBRUARY 1985

1936

LIVING GROUPS

Heave Ho!

When painters left their block and tackle, dormitory residents put it to use.

Offstreet Parking

ZBT / C. 1985

BURTON / JANUARY 1987

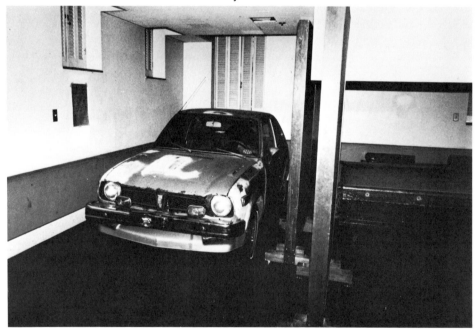

Genius

Residents of the dorms, returning from more or less strenuous vacations were greeted by the interesting sight of an old Ford coupe occupying the space formerly taken by the cute poles in the middle of the walk. Now, as every freshman knows, no two physical bodies can occupy the same space at the same time (seniors may not agree, but that is the accepted version); so that meant that the pole had been snapped off. Closer investigation revealed the pole in its proper position with reference to the ground, but occupying the interior of the car. In other words the car had been neatly impaled upon the post.

Came morning. Also a number of workmen. Rumor has it that it only took seven students to carry out the prank. One to watch and six to lift. Sheer brawn being all that was needed. Well, as we were saying, along came the Institute workmen. With a couple of big jacks, horses, and a truck load of planks. They used the lever principle, friction, and a number of other intricacies of mechanics. After a good hour of work the car was eased to a somewhat bumpy landing. On the INSIDE of the court.???

The Natives Are Revolting

Busloads of tourists regularly travel down Amherst Alley past some of the dormitories and fraternities to see the sights at MIT. Baker residents responded to one such invasion armed with bows and suction cup arrows, fencing foils, Star Trek phasers, and other "weapons."

BAKER / APRIL 1976

The Dorm Goblin

In the 1920s, the "Dorm Goblin" was responsible for many hacks. These often involved moving large objects.

A Ford chassis complete with its engine was hauled to the roof of the '93 Dormitory (part of East Campus).

Finding a Ford touring car improperly parked, the Dorm Goblin silently moved it into the basement of the '93 Dormitory where it was discovered the next morning completely intact and without a scratch. Twelve workers, four supervisors, and a tractor were used to remove it.

MARCH 1926

JANUARY 1926

Reprinted from *The Boston Herald* - May 28, 1928.

POLICE FIND COW ON ROOF OF
5-STORY M.I.T. DORMITORY

AMID CHEERS OF STUDENTS SHE IS
COAXED DOWN STAIRWAY TO STREET

Has anybody lost a brown and white old and decrepit knobbed-back cow? He will find one in the Cambridge city yard where she was taken yesterday by a member of the Cambridge police after a thrilling rescue from the roof of a Technology dormitory.

And here is the tale of the cow! Yesterday morning Patrolman Albert Waite of the Cambridge police department was patroling his beat in the Technology dormitory section. Meandering along, enjoying the morning air, he was startled by the sight of four students busily engaged in picking grass.

Nonplussed by such a spectacle, he asked an approaching student the reason for the grass plucking, thinking the while that the boys were performing an initiation stunt.

"Oh, some of the boys have got a cow on top of dormitory No. 93," came the answer.

USES VERNACULAR

"What the ——"! ejaculated the startled patrolman, and started on the hotfoot for dormitory No. 93.

Now dormitory No. 93 is a new five-story brick building on Ames street, and its roof is enclosed by a high railing on all sides. Officer Waite, taking the stairs on the run, found bossy munching contentedly on the fresh green grass, surrounded by a group of admiring students, very much at home in her brick and concrete pasture.

"Who brought that cow up here?" the patrolman inquired.

Loud cheers.

"How did she get up here?" he persisted.

"Up the stairs," came the merry rejoinder.

"Well down the stairs she'll go and right now," concluded the officer.

WILLING TO GO UP BUT NOT DOWN

But how? Everyone seemed to remember at once that at some time or other it was brought to their attention that a cow could climb stairs but that the same animal would refuse to descend them.

"She's going down the way she came up and no other way," proclaimed the patrolman, and his ultimatum was greeted with cheers.

And so the retreat from the roof began!

First a stout rope was placed around her neck and she was given a fresh supply of grass. With more held in front of her, the march of the bovine squadron, headed by Officer Waite and Asst. Supt. of Buildings Frederick Hartwell got under way.

GETS TEMPERAMENTAL

All went well until the top of the first stairway was reached. Then bossy asserted her feminine prerogative and refused to descend. With the air of a temperamental diva, she bellowed, mooed, kicked and endeavored to get her short-horns in action.

Cheer on cheer re-echoed through No. 93. At every landing crowds of students were gathered, yelling advice to the 20 or more at the roof entrance. Outside were gathered several hundred more echoing each bellow with a yell.

At last, with five students in front of bossy, and with twice that number providing the leverage in the rear, she was eased gently, despite her active protestations, down the first few steps.

"Look out! She's slipping! Hold her back!" shouted the boys in front. "Grab her tail, we can't hold her," they implored.

Willing hands grabbed bossy's tail, and whether frightened or merely grateful she refrained from kicking or butting on the way to first landing. There she was met with libations of water and fresh rations of grass by admiring students and followed the tempting herbage to the next landing.

MET BY DELEGATION AT FOOT OF STAIRS

This process was continued down the five stories to the entrance. Delegations met the strange procession at every landing. Bossy was cheered, Officer Waite was cheered, Supt. Hartwell was cheered and the lowly cow herders were cheered.

At last the solid terra firma was in sight. Grouped around the entrance were hundreds of students and a mob of kids. Pandemonium broke loose. The crowd howled in glee and cheered and yelled, but the cowboys were, it seemed, getting more enjoyment out of the situation themselves, for they left their charge in the hands of Officer Waite and sat down on the steps, holding their sides with laughter.

With a parting roar from the crowd and accompanied by the small army of youngsters, Officer Waite, top cowboy extraordinary, started his mile trek to the city yards, leading the docile bossy by a rope.

MAY 1928

LIVING GROUPS

This thirty-five-foot telegraph pole was found threaded through Atkinson Hall in Senior House—six workers and a tractor were required to remove it.

JANUARY 1928

 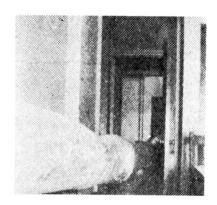

The Tech - February 18, 1929

Dorm Goblin Inspires Telephones With Music

Telephones in the new dorms were put to a strange use on Friday night when upon lifting off the receiver one could hear the music of a radio. The receiver was a perfect loud speaker and filled each room with melodies. The dorm goblin had been playing with the telephones after the dormitory telephone service had been discontinued at 11 o'clock. He had succeeded in connecting the wires so that all could enjoy the sounds emitted from one radio set.

CLASSES

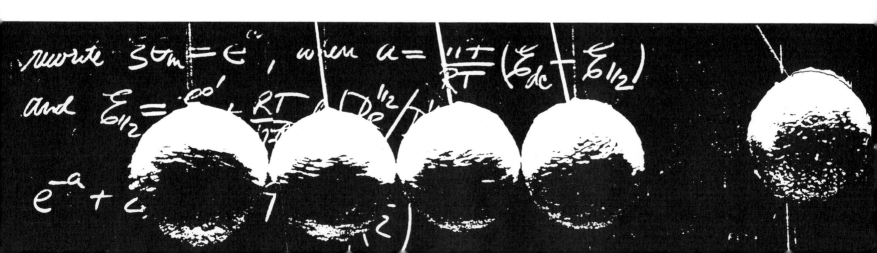

Can You Say "Turbojet"?

The turbojet display from the third floor of Building 33 was moved to the lecture hall on the second floor of Building 35 where unified engineering lectures were held.

THE UNIFRIED HACKERS / APRIL 1987

A Classy Exam

Chalkboard Gremlin

This device gave a student radio control of a movable chalkboard in the large lecture hall in Building 10.

1981

Classroom Reversal

One morning students arriving for a lecture in room 2-190 found the 199 seats turned around to face the rear of the room. The seats in this lecture hall are bolted to the floor with two bolts under each armrest and connected together into long rows.

NOVEMBER 1982

Aerodynamics Exercise

Copies of this assignment were left by the entrance to a lecture hall where class handouts were usually placed. Students dutifully picked up copies as they entered the room for their physics lecture. The "assignment" called for the construction of a paper airplane with instructions to launch when the classroom clock read exactly 11:15. At the specified time, hundreds of paper airplanes flew at the lecturer.

JACK E. FLOREY / OCTOBER 1985

MASSACHUSETTS INSTITUTE OF TECHNOLOGY
Physics Department

Physics 8.01   October 25, 1985

ASSIGNMENT No. 7.1
(Do 11:15 a.m., Friday, October 25)

Reading Assignment for Week no. 7:
Review of airplane tossing technique, Chapter 22.5.
Advanced folding technique, Chapter 22.7.
Infra-red tracking and guidance techniques, Chapter 23.2.

Material Covered in Lecture this week:

Friday, October 25	Ready
Friday, October 25	Aim
Friday, October 25	Fire
Monday, October 28	First Aid

(special topic: treatment of paper cuts.)

Special Reminder:
The final exam in paper airplane construction and launch will be held (during the lecture time) on Friday, October 25. You will be held responsible for the material covered in chapters 22-3 (i.e. this homework,

Problem 7.1-1: Paper airplane construction.
If you don't know how to make one by now, you're probably beyond hope, but as Airplane construction is only a minor subtopic, I have included a diagram of the necessary folds as well as the final product. You may use this paper. Extra credit will be given for creative designs.

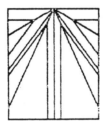

Figure 7.1.2: A paper airplane

Figure 7.1.1: Folding diagram

Problem 7.1-2: Paper Airplane Launching.
As its name suggests, this step involves the launching of the planes designed in problem 7.1-2. The goal is for the entire paper airplane fleet to impact the general vicinity of Professor Meyer at a given time. This involves proper launching technique to maximize the distance function with respect to force, and thus, the range of the airplane. Completing this problem will necessitate drawing a free-body diagram of the plane, including air resistance and lift, as well as a rad 3 measurement to within 3 microns (1 micron = 1×10^{-6}m) accuracy) of the distance from your seat to the stage. As our goal is to minimize error, we must make many simultaneous trials of this experiment. Hint: throw it at the professor.

IMPORTANT NOTE: The launch is to take place at precisely 11:15 a.m. according to the room clock. Please have your equipment ready to by then. Fnord.

Clack . . . Clack . . . Clack . . .

A large version of a collision ball apparatus was installed in a lecture hall one night.

"Children Will Play"
in German Class

Members of Professor Kurrelmeyer's German class the other day got together and decided that something appropriate must be done to bring the season to a fitting close. The day before the class met, the conspirators held a convocation, and forthwith, just before class each member showed up with a burden that looked as if it had been secured in a raid on Woolworth's. Placing their loads on the Professor's desk, the chairs were then arranged in a circle, kindergarten style, and the children then took their seats to await teacher's arrival.

He soon showed up, and with his sweet smile received the gifts tendered him. They included a beautiful 10-cent straw hat adorned with a brilliant red ribbon, a lolly-pop of considerable area, a toy chicken, a celluloid fish, and numerous packages daintily tied with ribbon. Special presentation was made by one of the class of an alphabet which was the result of thesis work in the course of which he had discovered the fact that there were certain letters never to be used, and others that required more than ordinary use. This alphabet was minus an "F," and "C" and "P" were underlined. The applause following this presentation was rather more inspired, than necessary.

Professor Kurrelmeyer completed the session by delivering to his kindergarten a lecture on degradation of the morals of the present youth.

THE TECH

Saturday classes are the bane of many people's existence. Some accept them as fate, but not so for a group of enterprising young freshmen. They had an E 12 class, scheduled for 9:00 Saturday morning. They went all right . . . but by the time the third week rolled around they decided they had had enough. Last Saturday they showed up . . . dressed in bathrobes and pajamas.

* * * *

ANECDOTE REVEALS OLD TECH SPIRIT

Boylston Street Students Take Half of Class Period To Enter Lecture Room

"Tech Spirit" of the good old days at the school on Bolyston street has been brought to light through a story told of the late Professor of the Physics Department. The professor heartily disliked the frequent interruptions of his lectures by the tardy arrival of certain sleepy students, and though he claimed he would never shut the lecture room door in a man's face, he would close and lock the door as near five minutes after the hour as the last man in sight would permit.

One day the professor stalked into the hall, and glanced around amazedly; not a single student was there for the lecture! Promptly at five minutes after the bell he went to the door to lock the entire class out, but a man walked in unconcernedly just before he reached it, followed immediately by several more, all taking their time as though nothing were at all out of the ordinary. Professor Cross glanced down the hall to make sure no one was in sight, but along came five or six others, followed by couple after couple, each coming into view as the man ahead entered the room. The astounded professor would not go back on his word, but sat down resignedly to wait the full twenty-five minutes that it took for his class to accumulate.

ART AND EXHIBITS

MIT has several galleries and a museum that exhibit a wide range of art and technology. In addition, there are sculptures, murals, and many smaller exhibits throughout the campus exploring topics such as MIT history, personalities, and technological developments. Exposure to these exhibits has inspired many hacks. . . .

"No Knife"

During the first exhibit in the List Galleries in the Wiesner Arts and Media Building, students installed their own addition to a contemporary art exhibit.

JAMES E. TETAZOO / MARCH 1985

NO KNIFE

A STUDY IN MIXED MEDIA EARTH TONES, NUMBER THREE.

Realized by James Tetazoo   December 1984

The artist's *mode d'emploi* relies upon minimalist kinematic methods; space and time are frozen in a staid reality of restrained sexuality. Temporary occasionalism, soon overcome throughout by symbolic nihility, pervades our earliest perception of the work. An overturned throwaway obelisk functions as symbolic pedestal; the work rests upon a manifestation of grey toned absence. Epicurean imagery is employed most effectively by Tetazoo; the glass, the porcelain, the plastic move in conflicting directions and yet are joined in a mood of stark pacifism. The sterile lateralism of the grouped utensils (*sans* knife), conveys a sense of eternal ennui, framed within the subtle ambience of discrete putrefaction. The casual formalism of the place setting draws upon our common internal instinct of existential persistence to unify us with the greater consciousness of human bondage.

High Class Art

The circular reading room of Barker Engineering Library is 70 feet in diameter with a 65-foot-high domed ceiling, the inside of the great dome. Students suspended their own sculpture approximately 45 feet above the floor.

FOURTH EAST, EAST CAMPUS / C. 1979

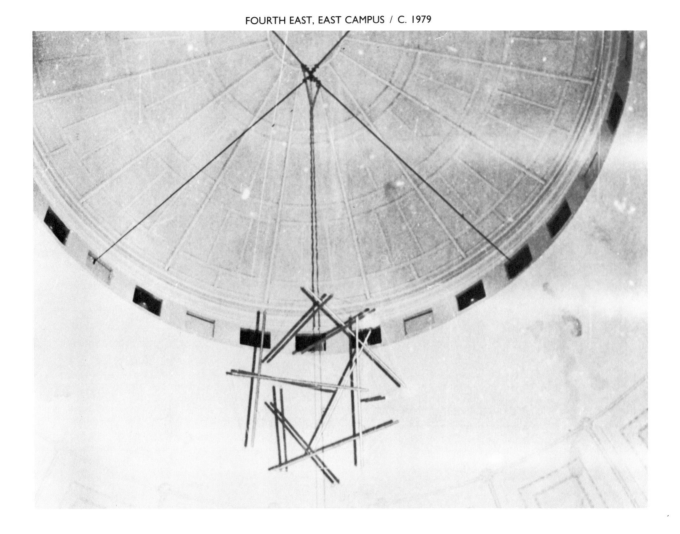

U.S.S. Tetazoo

The *U.S.S. Tetazoo* (a dime-store plastic model aircraft carrier) and a card with the ship's history was added to a Hart Nautical Galleries exhibit at a lightly attended midnight dedication.

JAMES E. TETAZOO / OCTOBER 1979

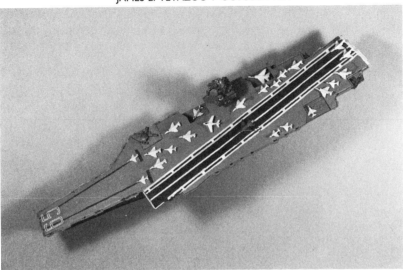

U.S.S. TETAZOO

Constructed in 423 B.C. by the Phoenician Turtle King Shii-Dawg, the Tetazoo's keel was laid 4 years later in Damascus.

During the Middle Ages she was put into drydock in Norfolk, Virginia until 1490 when she returned to Spain to show Christopher Columbo the route to the Americas under the new name "Ninny," later misspelled by Spanish hysterians. Running low on rum she detoured to Puerto Rico, where the wreck of the Santa Maria can be seen to this day.

In the early 1800's she became a privateer under Sir Harry Flashman, C.A.P., C.I.A., C.O.D.. Lost to the Swiss Navy in fierce combat in the Inside Straits, she remained in their possession until 1905, when she was given to the U.S. Navy as spoils from the Russo-Japanese War.

During WW II she served with distinction in the Atlantic, sinking 7 submarines, many of them enemy. Captained by James Tetazoo, Sr., she was named in his honor after he died while making a still from an old depth charge. To this day she serves with pride as the only (official) floating still in the U.S. Navy.

Lost Horizon

Transparent Horizon by Louise Nevelson was commissioned by the MIT Committee on the Visual Arts and installed near the Chemical Engineering Building in the fall of 1975. Students felt that the sculpture intruded on the East Campus courtyard and resented that the site was chosen without consulting dormitory residents.

In 1977 and 1978, East Campus residents buried *Transparent Horizon* with snow.

In the summer of 1981, *Transparent Horizon* was rededicated and a new plaque was installed.

JAMES E. TETAZOO / 1981

1984

1979

EXHIBITS

89

HAHVAHD

JOHNNY
RENTED
PORTABLE TOILETS
SERVICED

The little red brick school up Massachusetts Avenue from MIT has been the object of many hacks.

John Harvard's Brass Rat

John Harvard, sitting on his pedestal in Harvard Yard, proudly displayed his 1980 MIT class ring. The ring was cast in bronze in two parts scaled to the statue's proportions and then epoxied together on the statue. (Ironically, the artist who created the statue of John Harvard was Daniel Chester French, MIT class of 1871.)

THE SMILING SIX / MAY 1979

Johnny-on-the-Spot

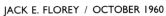

JACK E. FLOREY / OCTOBER 1960

Celebrity Kidnappings

In April 1940, DKE brothers, pretending to be Harvard students, met Eddie Anderson ("Rochester" on Jack Benny's radio shows) at the Providence airport and explained that they would drive him to the Harvard Freshman Smoker to avoid the crowds at the Boston Airport. Anderson was taken instead to a smoker at the DKE house at MIT and, after a while, told of the hoax and taken to Harvard.

Harvard students "attacked" the DKE house in retaliation on the next two evenings and "riots" ensued. MIT students claimed 22½ pairs of trousers, one pair of underwear, and a belt as trophies from the skirmishes.

The next night, an official car from Harvard waited in front of the Metropolitan Theater to transport Anderson to a reception. DKE brothers once again intercepted Anderson, this time backstage, escorted him out the back door to their car, and drove him to his reception.

On May 6, 1941, an MIT student, pretending to be a representative of Harvard, picked up burlesque queen Sally Rand at the Latin Quarter where she was performing. She was scheduled to entertain later that evening at a Harvard Freshman Smoker. Instead, she was brought to MIT, given a reception, and bestowed the title of "Associate Professor of Entertainment Engineering." Rand, who said that it was the nicest kidnapping she had ever experienced, was then delivered to the Sanders Theater for the Harvard Smoker.

Later that evening, Tech students escorted Yvette, a French singer, from the Harvard Smoker to the Chi Phi fraternity house. After singing for the brothers of Chi Phi and Fiji, she too was returned to Harvard.

Colonizing Harvard

In the spring of 1982, the newly elected MIT Undergraduate Association president and vice president conducted their first meeting. Vitalis hair tonic was distributed so that they could "share the grease." *Grease* is widely used by students to describe involvement in student government and student organizations, especially those organizations with offices on the fourth floor of the student center. Among students, the term *grease* usually implies a desire to wield power.

In April 1982, Harvard University's student government was in the throes of reorganization. The new MIT student government felt that the confusion at Harvard was a good opportunity for a hack. This article from the *Harvard Crimson* described the MIT student government's actions.

STUDENT LEADERS AT MIT CLAIM
HARVARD AS COLONY

BY JESSICA MARSHALL

Anyone who wonders just where to find the center of student authority at Harvard can now look to MIT.

Confronted with rumors that Harvard currently lacks a cohesive student government, the MIT Undergraduate Association last Thursday passed a resolution granting Harvard College colonial status and appointing sophomore Paula J. Van Lare colonial governor.

Van Lare said yesterday she does not expect any organized resistance from her new subjects. "Seeing the success Harvard has had organizing itself in the past, I sort of doubt it," she said.

MIT junior Kenneth H. Segel, president of the MIT student government, said yesterday giving Harvard colony status will be no problem, explaining that "basically everything can be reduced to an engineering problem." He added, "We'll probably let you move up to province status if you're good."

[Harvard] Dean of Students Archie C. Epps yesterday expressed surprise at the MIT takeover, saying, "I didn't realize that they learned anything about American government at MIT."

And associate professor of history Bradford Lee questioned the prudence of the move, observing that the invocation of colonial status "usually breeds an anti-colonial movement."

Confirming Lee's prediction, Andrew B. Herrmann '82—former chairman of Harvard's Student Assembly—called for "a 26-mile blockade around Harvard Square." Asked Herrmann, "What are they going to attack us with—calculators and slide rules? They don't even have a football team."

Harvard's new rulers include the leaders of the MIT Undergraduate Assembly elected in early March. Segel and his running mate, vice-president Kenneth J. Meltsner, also a junior, ran on the Gumby Party, whose motto is "Reason as a last resort." After their election, they found that the MIT student body "pretty much had their stuff together" and turned their sights to Harvard.

Besides governor Van Lare, the protectorate also includes sophomore William B. Coney, as secretary of defense, and Deren Hansen, as ambassador to extra-terrestrial civilizations. Van Lare said she expects to create other posts for her MIT friends.

Harvard's current Student Assembly Chairman Natasha Pearl '83, when informed that her powers had been usurped, dismissed MIT's gesture of munificence, saying her own unfunded government doesn't "want their sympathy, just their cash or personal checks."

The next fall, at the freshman picnic, an MIT hacking group, Commando Hacks, staged the abduction of the MIT Undergraduate Association president during his speech. The ransom note given to the MIT president demanded that Harvard be released from MIT's tyrannical rule. A banner demanding, "FREE HARVARD," appeared after the abduction.

HAHVAHD

Harvard Stadium has served as an arena for many hacks—some successful, some less so. A hack in the Harvard Stadium is very difficult to execute; the Harvard Police patrol the stadium and any equipment used must escape detection by the grounds crew.

MIT Wins the Harvard-Yale Football Game

During the break following a touchdown in the first quarter of the 1982 Harvard-Yale game, a black weather balloon emerged from the turf on the forty-six yard line. The balloon inflated to six feet in diameter before bursting in a cloud of talcum powder. (After extensive negotiations, the device was given to the MIT Museum.)

DKE

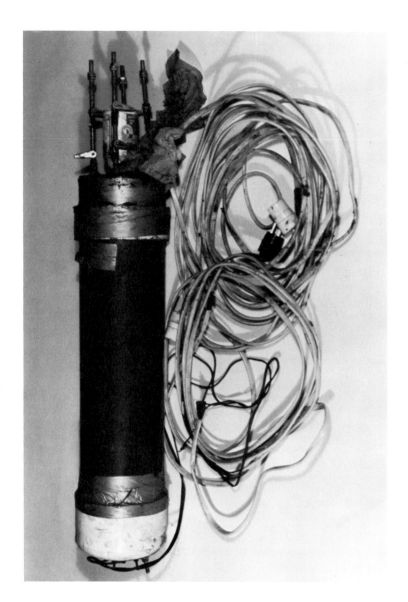

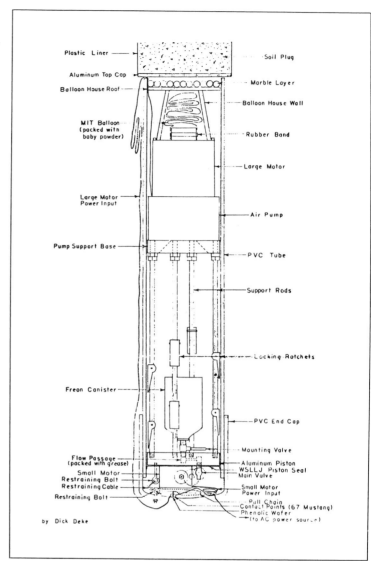

Plastic Liner —
Aluminum Top Cap —
Balloon House Roof —

MIT Balloon
(packed with
baby powder)

Large Motor
Power Input —

Pump Support Base —

Freon Canister —

Flow Passage
(packed with grease)
Small Motor
Restraining Bolt
Restraining Cable
Restraining Bolt —

Soil Plug —
Marble Layer
Balloon House Wall
Rubber Band
Large Motor
Air Pump
PVC Tube
Support Rods
Locking Ratchets
PVC End Cap
Mounting Valve
Aluminum Piston
WSLLJ Piston Seal
Main Valve
Small Motor
Power Input
Pull Chain
Contact Points (67 Mustang)
Phenolic Wafer
(to AC power source)

by Dick Deke

The media attention focused on the balloon hack overshadowed the fact that the Undergraduate Association and THA organized two other successful hacks at the same game. Between the half-time shows of the Yale and Harvard bands, the MIT Marching Band paraded onto the field and lay down forming the letters "MIT" with their bodies. They made it past the security guards by dressing in the sweatshirts and white pants of the Yale band.

In the last quarter, colored cards were handed out to Harvard fans in the stands. Told that the cards would spell "BEAT YALE," the fans dutifully raised them as instructed not realizing that the 1,134 cards actually spelled "MIT."

All Tech Men Wear Batteries

Before the Harvard-Yale football game in 1948, eight MIT students planted primer cord (an explosive used to ignite dynamite) beneath the turf of the Harvard football field spelling out "MIT" in fifteen-foot letters. A grounds-keeper discovered the ends of the wires hidden under a pile of trash beneath the grandstands. The primer cord was removed, but the exposed ends of the wire were left in place so the hackers would not realize that their plan had been discovered. Just before the game, a student with dry cells under his jacket appeared near the wires and was apprehended. The hacker's explanation: "All Tech men carry batteries for emergencies."

In honor of this event, many Tech students wore batteries under their jackets during the next week. The Boston newspapers erroneously reported that a crater would have been blown in the field. Tests performed during the planning of the hack, however, showed that the primer cord would have created only a shallow furrow.

Curses, Foiled Again

A few days before the 1978 Harvard-Yale game, some Yale students were caught killing the grass on the field in a large "Y." While repairing the turf, the grounds crew discovered a remote control spray paint system buried under the field. When triggered, the device would have painted a large "MIT" on the field.

Harvard Again Outfoxed By Beaver Pranksters

A flustered Crimson football team walked over not one, but two, rivals in its first game of the present season last Saturday in the Harvard bowl, both literally and figuratively speaking.

When John Harvard's gridiron proteges romped out on to the playing field, they saw, not eleven menacing, scowling football greats, but three brown letters—M.I.T.—burned into the otherwise flawless turf by a band of Technology's loyal sons.

The M.I.T. jinx had some effect, however, for the Crimson had a tough time eking out a two touchdown victory over underdog Amherst.

Voo Doo - March 1961

HAHVAHD

HARVARD BRIDGE

250
SMOOTS

Technology Bridge

Causing much confusion with visitors, the bridge that crosses the Charles River at MIT is called the Harvard Bridge. It was named after John Harvard for whom the small red brick college in Cambridge had earlier been named. When the bridge was opened in 1891, MIT was located in Boston. The controversy over the bridge's name began in 1916 when MIT opened its Cambridge campus.

When the Harvard Bridge was closed for renovations in 1924, 1949, and 1986, proposals were submitted to rename the bridge for MIT. Each time, however, the proposed name change did not make it through the long political process required. Many at MIT, feeling that the bridge was poorly designed, did not want it named for MIT.

The Boston Herald - November 1, 1946

TECH'S BRIDGE   *By Dahl*

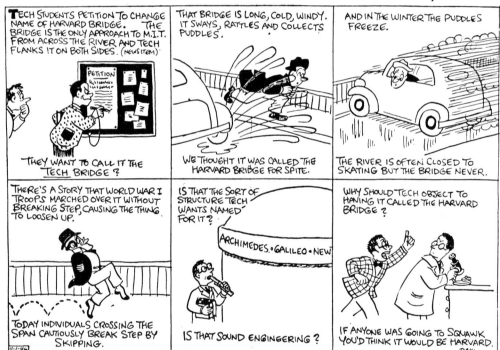

While the Harvard Bridge was closed in 1949 for renovations, the "Harvard Bridge Closed" sign was replaced by Tech students.

At the opening ceremony later that year, Massachusetts Governor Paul A. Dever led a motorcade toward the bridge. Just before he reached it, a convertible containing ten members of *The Tech* staff, a brass band, and two clowns pulled in front of the governor's limousine and started across the bridge. The police stopped the convertible, but the pranksters' car was the second to cross the newly rebuilt bridge.

A New Unit of Length

The official length of the Harvard Bridge is 364.4 Smoots plus one ear. Distances on the bridge are indicated with a colored paint mark every Smoot and a number every ten Smoots. Biannually, the pledge class of Lambda Chi Alpha repaints the markings with a new color. The police have come to accept the Smoot marks. In fact, they use the markers to indicate locations when filing accident reports. After the bridge was rebuilt in the late 1980s, the Smoot markings reappeared and the tradition continued.

The story of these markings as told by Oliver Reed Smoot, Jr., '62:

As all who walked the bridge in those days will remember, it was difficult, especially in the rain, sleet, snow, and fog of which Boston gets its share, to know how much further you had to go to get to the Institute. So in October 1958, O'Connor . . . devised the idea of marking off the bridge in pledge lengths. Scanning the assembled pledge class, he determined that I had the short end of the stick.

As with many pledge tasks, there was an easy way out if a little ingenuity was exercised—namely use a string. In any case, Pete, Gordon, Nate and Bill agreed to help and we set off with the paint, chalk, etc. Unfortunately, a brother in the class of '61 thought this task was so hilarious that he accompanied us. With him there, we had no choice but to do the actual measurements. I can tell you that even then I could not do the equivalent of 365 push-ups, so much of the way I was carried or dragged.

Luckily for the five of us, we were cold sober; in any case, when an MDC [Metropolitan District Commission] black van appeared at about the 300 mark, we cut for the dark recesses of the Great Court and waited for them to leave.

HARVARD BRIDGE

109

HARVARD BRIDGE

110

HARVARD BRIDGE

111

HARVARD BRIDGE

112

HARVARD BRIDGE

113

HARVARD BRIDGE

HOAXES

The Great Snowjob

Reprinted from *The Tech* - January 12, 1968.

'SNOW IN BAKER' FOOLS NATION

BY MARK BOLOTIN

"In the second floor shower rooms at Baker House, they threw the windows wide open and turned the hot showers on full blast. From the showers poured a thick plume of steam. From the open windows came a below-zero icy blast. The experiment was designed to determine what happens when one meets the other."

So claimed Tuesday's edition of the *Boston Herald-Traveler,* which fell for a hoax perpetrated by Baker residents. The front-page story, with accompanying picture, concluded that "Steam + Icy Air = Snow."

In reality, there was a considerable amount of snow on the floor of the john, although certainly not the six inches claimed by the *Herald-Traveler.* Despite the claims of the paper, the snow was not artificially created by the students; it was merely brought in from outside to build a snowman. Unfortunately, the snow was too dry to pack, so the showers were turned on very hot. (It is true that warm water will soften snow enough to make it packable—no hoax.)

However, with the hot showers on, it became necessary to open a window to cool the room off. Suddenly, the room was filled with fog, caused by cold air meeting steam. One member of the crowd decided that this fantastic effect would be the basis for a great hack—a claim that they had created snow.

The newspaper—and most of Boston—fell for it. The paper finally realized that it had been fooled, when besieged with complaints. Nobody else was able to obtain snow by this method.

Latest responses to the hoax took two extremes. The most common reaction was the reply of one MIT student: "Anybody knows that if you mix hot water and cold air, the only thing you'll get is a cold shower." Nevertheless, one perpetrator of the hoax hoped that they might really be able to create snow. If the room is cold enough and with the right type nozzle on the shower . . .

News of the supposed creation of snow in Baker House spread far beyond Boston. The news story was picked up by the Associated Press wire service and carried to newspapers and televisions across the nation.

It has been verified that the story was reported in newspapers in Georgia and New Jersey. Television stations in Atlanta, Ga., also presented the story.

According to . . . a Baker resident who helped organize the hoax, parents of several other Bakerites called Cambridge to report that local papers carried the story. He added it is likely that the story crossed the country, but that not all reports of its coverage have reached Cambridge.

IAP Person-napping

The IAP person, a life-size painting on cardboard that symbolized Independent Activities Period in the late seventies, was kidnapped and a ransom note with a photo was left. A reply was printed in *Tech Talk* on February 1, 1978. This satisfied the kidnappers and the IAP person was returned unharmed.

JAMES E. TETAZOO / JANUARY 1978

We have THE IAP man. HE will diE unLess THEse deMands ARE MEt By MidnighT THE Last day OF iaP:
* iaP WIll BE eXTEnded 30 DAYs
* tHE ILetteR "Q" wIll be STRicken fRom THe AlPhaBet
* all InstitUTE CourseS shall be taught in the furlong stOne FortnigT fsf syStEM
* all classes WIll Be taught in CoBol
* 16th wEek dROP daTe
* PRe|Sident WiEsneR mUst eat a

Ilnch at Lobdell
* light mUst obSerVE the 55 MPh limit.

WE will Be awaiting rePly In tech taLK.

Missing Person

Someone over the weekend stole the five-foot cardboard symbol of MIT's Independent Activities Period—a winged figure riding a bicycle—from the IAP Office, 7-108, and left a ransom note demanding, among other things, that the speed of light be slowed to the energy-saving, federally mandated highway safety limit of 55 miles an hour.

The abductors said the cardboard symbol—referred to in the note as the "IAP man" but known officially at MIT as the "IAP person"—will die unless a series of demands are met by midnight, Wednesday, Feb. 1, the last day of this year's IAP.

Joel Orlen, executive director in the Office of the Provost and chairman of the IAP Planning Committee, said the IAP person is much cherished by IAP personnel and Institute officials are prepared to meet at least some of the demands in order to ensure that he/she/it is released unharmed. The figure was made by a freelance artist a year ago as an IAP symbol and the likeness appeared on most IAP literature a year ago.

The ransom note was made from letters cut out of magazines and newspapers, pasted crudely on two sheets of paper and delivered to the office of President Jerome B. Wiesner and the IAP Office. A Polaroid color photo accompanied the note showing the figure trussed in ropes and being held by someone in a hood mask.

(For some reason, the abductors did not send in the note itself, only a Xerox copy of it.)

One demand—that IAP be extended 30 days—was immediately agreed to by Orlen.

"Each Sunday for the next 30 weeks will be an IAP day," Orlen said, "and everyone at MIT should feel free to pursue whatever independent activity s/he desires, except for those assigned to regular shifts and graduate students working on theses, which are usual IAP rules."

Orlen said slowing the speed of light to 55mph could prove a boon to physicists who, in doing experiments, often find that light moves too fast anyway. Instructions are being prepared.

Orlen also agreed to the demand that the letter "q" be dropped from the alphabet. He said it will be replaced with the letters "kw" and urged the abductors to release the IAP person kwuickly.

Another demand was that the Institute convert measurements to the furlong/stone/fortnight system. Orlen said the demand will be met as soon as the metric system has been fully installed—"probably 100 years from now."

One demand—that President Wiesner eat lunch at Lobdell Dining Room—already has been met, Orlen said.

"He ate there three weeks ago and we presume that counts," he said.

Orlen rejected two demands—that all classes be taught in cobol and that the drop date be set at 16 weeks.

"People can teach classes at MIT in whatever color they choose," Orlen said. "As for the 16-week drop date, it simply doesn't go far enough."

Elephas pseudotherias

The article on the following page was printed in the April 1984 issue of *Technology Review.*

In the October 1984 issue of *Technology Review,* the editor gave the following account of the "woolly mammoth" story:

OUR SHAGGY ELEPHANT

It all began more than a year ago in an MIT science writing class. A talented undergraduate submitted for possible use in *Technology Review* a beautifully written account of the discovery in the U.S.S.R. of ova from a woolly mammoth frozen in arctic ice. This long-preserved material was eventually used, according to the account, to breed a mammoth-elephant hybrid called a "mammontelephas," from the Russian mammonth and the Greek elephas, with a biological name Elephas pseudotherias. The principals in this scientific achievement were said to be a Dr. Sverbighooze Nikhiphorovich Yasmilov of the University of Irkutsk and a Dr. James Creak of MIT.

It took us a few hours to appreciate the skill with which Diana ben-Aaron had turned an assignment in science writing into a brilliant exercise in parody, and soon enough we resolved to share ben-Aaron's achievement with our readers in celebration of All Fools' Day. Hence the feature on page 85 of our April 1984 issue.

But, as Robert Cooke, science editor of the *Boston Globe,* noted in a front page feature late last summer, "Some folks there are who cannot take a joke." For early last May we were startled to find Diana's science nonsense taken seriously by the *Chicago Tribune* and subsequently by a number of other newspapers that subscribe to the *Tribune*'s syndicate service. Eventually *Family Weekly,* a Sunday supplement distributed in over 350 U.S. newspapers, carried the story. Meanwhile, this editor has sought to explain the April Fools' Day tradition to a biologist at the Chettiar Research Centre of Madras; and Charles Ball of the MIT News Office found himself struggling to tell a Paris journalist, "N'est pas vrai!" in his best French accent.

Retrobreeding the Woolly Mammoth

L ast year in the Soviet Union, Dr. Sverbighooze Nikhiphorovich Yasmilov, head of veterinary research at the University of Irkutsk, got hold of some cells—including some ova, or egg cells—from a young woolly mammoth found frozen in Siberia. Although the cytoplasm—the material forming the bulk of the cell—was unhealthy, Yasmilov was able to extract the nuclei. He implanted these into viable cytoplasm from elsewhere in the mammoth.

Yasmilov continued his investigations by sending some cells to Dr. James Creak of M.I.T. for testing. Creak heated the DNA from the mammoth ova until it dissociated into short lengths of code. After a number of false starts, he tried mixing it with a similarly prepared solution of the DNA of elephant sperm. The sections of elephant and mammoth code that matched "zipped themselves together," according to Creak, "as DNA is wont to do." This "paired DNA," representing the code common to elephants and woolly mammoths, was centrifuged off, leaving a residue of code that differed between the two species. The difference was less than 4.3 percent.

This started Creak thinking. The elephant has 56 chromosomes, and the mammoth has 58. "Now look at the donkey and the horse," Creak explained. "The donkey has 62 chromosomes and the horse has 64, yet horses and donkeys can mate to produce mules and hinnies. So is it unreasonable to suggest an elephant-mammoth hybrid?"

Creak communicated the good news at once to Yasmilov, who promptly set to work trying to fuse the nuclei from the mammoth ova, in their new cytoplasm, with sperm from an Asian elephant bull. As Creak points out, this delicate work requires highly skilled technicians. "In this profession," he observed, "people who can work with DNA and have it come out whole are traded like major-league baseball players, and they are even more valuable because the stakes are higher."

Creak expressed concern about the state of experimental science in general. "Some scientists like to proceed in small, carefully thought-out steps. They are like accountants, and might as well be," he complained. "I see science as high adventure, with enormous risks. Of course, the rewards are commensurately high if the gamble comes off."

Yasmilov attempted to artificially inseminate the mammoth ova with elephant sperm over 60 times before achieving fusion in eight samples. The resulting cell clusters were implanted in the wombs of Indian elephant cows. The timing of implantation is tricky, as the elephant cow must be in heat and proceed directly to the pregnant state after the embryo is implanted. Most of the elephant cows spontaneously miscarried, but two of the surrogate mothers carried to term, giving birth to the first known elephant-mammoth hybrids.

Scientists have classified the calves as woolly mammoths according to two criteria. First, the yellow-brown hair that covered the newborn did not fall out after birth, as it does in "modern" elephants. Second, the calves' jaw structure closely resembles that of mammoths.

Finding a scientific name for the young mammoth-elephant hybrid has been difficult. Professor Herman Hoffman of M.I.T.'s Linguistics Department suggests the word "mammontelephas" (it's singular), which he coined from the Russian *mammonth*, or mammoth, and the Greek *elephas*, or elephant. "It has—dare I say it?—almost a Byzantine ring," said Hoffman. Creak proposed the biological name *Elephas pseudotherias*, which would make the animals members of the Theria class of mammals. He added that the young mammontelephases belong to the order Proboscidea, having a long proboscis, or snout. It is not known whether the Russian scientists have classified the animals.

Unfortunately for those who had hoped to breed the two mammals, both are male. They are probably sterile anyway, Creak points out. Mules are almost invariably sterile because they end up with an odd number of chromosomes—31 (from the donkey parent) plus 32 (from the horse parent), making a total of 63. The 63 chromosomes in the mule's body cells divide randomly into 31 or 32 in the gametes, or germ cells. When two mules mate, the pairs of germ cells are so unevenly matched that the chromosomes simply cannot pair up. In fact, the Roman expression for "once in a blue moon" was *cum mula peperit*—"when the mule foals."

Although they will not reach adult size for another 25 years, the new mammoth calves have already exhibited extraordinary toughness by surviving the bitter cold of Irkutsk. They are being kept in an outdoor enclosure, and their reaction to the local weather conditions is being carefully monitored.

Mindful of the elephants used by Hannibal and Alexander the Great in cold climes, Yasmilov plans to train the mammontelephases to earn their keep when they reach adulthood. They could help pull immobilized convoy trucks out of the snowdrifts on the trans-Siberian highway. This is now a troublesome task, as the machinery employed to do the job may freeze in the bitter cold. The mammontelephases could also be used for logging, and there may even be a job on the trans-Siberian pipeline. —*Diana ben-Aaron* □ *April 1, 1984*

It's Not Whether You Win or Lose . . .

The Karoso Club was formed in the fall of 1950. In fact, the game Karoso did not exist at all and the club was actually a hoax. To sustain the guise of a student activity, the members held meetings and pretended to arrange intercollegiate tournaments. The Karoso Club was finally exposed as a hoax in February 1951 by a reporter from *The Tech*.

The following article describing the game was published in *The Tech Engineering News* shortly before the exposé in *The Tech*:

. . . AND NOW KAROSO

BY ANDREW BROWDER, '53

Of all the games of skill with which men of the western world have traditionally tried their wits, the two foremost are unquestionably chess and checkers. The former is now far more widely played than many people might believe, and in fact has had more literature published about it in the United States than any other game; the latter, once very popular, is now rarely played to the extent chess is. Among the devotees of both games, there often comes a point where the game seems exhausted of interest, and they turn to other diversions. Thus, the great master Capablanca once issued a statement to the effect that he had completely mastered the game of chess, that there was no more interest in it. Another great master, Emmanuel Lasker, perhaps the greatest chess player who ever lived, made checkers interesting by adding a few new concepts (he called the resulting game lasker). While neither Capablanca nor Lasker stopped playing chess professionally, both of them devoted more and more time to games such as lasker, Wei-Chi (better known by its Japanese name of Go), and Karoso. Incidentally, these three games in recent years have become the especial favorite of scientists and mathematicians. Go today stands much higher in point of number of active players than either lasker or Karoso. It is the latter, however, that seems destined to be the leading strategical game of the future.

Wei-Chi was said to be invented by the Chinese Emperor Shun (2255–2206 B.C.). Other legends attribute it to one U, who invented it for the Emperor Kieh Kwei, about four hundred years later. Whatever its origin, by the tenth century B.C. it was widely known and played, as witnessed by its frequent mention in literature of that period. In the eighth century A.D. Wei-Chi was brought to Japan, where it was called Go, by which name it has come to Europe and America. Go is a game of far more strategic depth than chess, although much simpler to learn. It is the national game of Japan, the only country in which exists a class of professional Go players, who generally earn their living by teaching. In fact, there are nine distinct classes of professional Go masters, the ninth class, now called Honinbo after the first champion, having been attained by only a few players in history. It is said that the finest Occidental players are at best still inferior to masters of the second rank. This game has recently been undergoing a tremendous growth in popularity in America among the relatively small group of players who take such games very seriously. Americans also like to play two minor variants of Go, known as Go Moku, and Ni Nuki.

Players of lasker differ from those of Go and Karoso in that, besides spelling their game with a lower-case letter, they approach the problem of finding new resources in games by modifying an existing game, rather than breaking entirely new ground. Lasker introduces into checker science a conservation of energy principle; that is, pieces captured are not removed from play, but remain as potential forces. There is no space here to go any further into this fascinating game; anyone wishing to learn more concerning the tactics and strategy of this more subtle and exciting mutant of the genus checkers can probably find lasker players at any checker of chess club, including that at M.I.T.

It will be the chief purpose of this article to discuss the origin and development of Karoso, the third important board game after chess and checkers. The father of Karoso was a Polish scientist and man of letters of the late nineteenth century.

When I. Boslevetsky, dean of Krakow chess players and a locally prominent mathematician, weary of the cliches of nineteenth century chess play, turned to the resources of his own mind to form a new and daring experiment in games of skill, he did not choose to elaborate further on the rococo ornateness of traditional chess. He simplified.

In brief, Boslevetsky first reduced the number of pieces from sixteen on a side to four. He discarded the old differentiation of mobility as a function of the design of the specific piece, the foundation of chess, and substituted newer, more fluid concepts. In the end, he achieved a game in which the object of play had become a subtle regeometrizing of permutations on pieces and squares. This he called Bosspiel.

Theoretically, it seemed at first that the game could be mathematically formulated by use of the theory of transfinite rings, then undergoing the initial stages of its development. But the computations were of incredible difficulty. After long efforts to crystallize the theory involved, Boslevetsky abandoned the effort, satisfied that it would provide endless problems to the practical player. As it turned out, Karoso's patron saint discovered that Bosspiel, not only imperfectible in the large but too extensive for the human mind to deal with, was not playable.

Thus was born and died Bosspiel, a game played only in one man's imagination, but nevertheless important. For it is Boslevetsky's simplification of this game that we play today as Karoso.

Karoso was scarcely known outside Poland for many years after its invention; in fact, it was not until after the first World War that the game attained a following in every important state in Europe, and in the United States and Canada. In the early 1920's, Karoso had a short-lived burst of popularity in the United States, particularly in New York City. Today one might search the major chess clubs in vain to find two people who play Karoso, although he might find many who remember the great Karoso tournaments of 1923 and 1924. These tournaments, great events in the development of the game, were nevertheless financial failures. Since that time, no major international tournaments have been held, and until the years following the second World War, Karoso was in decline. In the past several years, though, more people have been introduced to Karoso than ever before. Returning GI's brought the knowledge back that they had acquired in France, in England, even in Italy—significantly, not in Germany. In 1947 a national tournament was held under the auspices of the Sheridan Square Karoso Club in New York, and the winner, Dave Berk, was declared United States champion. In the past two years, several important universities have founded Karoso clubs, whose ultimate purpose will be to form an intercollegiate Karoso league. Important among these is M.I.T.

Karoso is an easy game to learn, difficult to play well, impossible to truly master. In these respects it, the newest of significant strategic games, is not unlike Go, said to be the oldest. The basic ideas of both games may be quickly picked up by watching, but the strategy of experts seems fantastically deep to the uninitiated.

Karoso is played on a standard sixty-four square checker board, with three uniform, undistinguished pieces, which both players move alternately, usually one at a time. From this description, the total number of positions possible must seem at first to be very small. However, when one realizes that a single square defines nine discrete positions, and that a piece may be moved onto any of these or onto points or lines of intersection, it becomes readily apparent that the opposite is the case. In fact, the number of positions available is about 1600^6, a number large enough so that a Swahili savage wishing to notch it up would require a tally stick reaching from Krakow to the star Θ Centauri, over sixty-five light years away! This number represents the total number of points on the board which a Karoso piece may occupy, 1600, to the power of the number of pieces (each piece may play two roles, called "yerd" and "thortle," so that there are in effect six pieces), an approximation to the permutation of 1600 things taken six at a time. A word about these words, yerd and thortle, as well as the expression, "studge," heard so often in play. These are nonsense words invented by the great English player Cunningham to take the place of the original Polish words, unpronounceable to many English and American players, and having no particular useful meaning other than in relation to the game.

Karoso's extreme flexibility, which makes it more popular with some people than others, is also the obstacle to complete mathematical formulation. While simpler than Bosspiel, the determinants necessary for the evaluation of a position can be solved in a reasonable length of time only with the largest digital computers now in operation, and apparently the commercial value of such a project is not sufficient to induce the owners of such machines to devote them to this high purpose.

Trashing Trash TV

Reprinted from *The Tab* - March 14, 1989.

MOUTH TRAP

BY BRUCE SYLVESTER

When archconservative TV talk show host Morton Downey, Jr. takes the stage at the Opera House this Saturday, chances are one of the last local people he'll want to see is his recent TV guest, mild-mannered Christopher Coon, age 20.

Wide-eyed Christopher Coon knew he was in unfriendly territory with a tough spot to defend—sexual or any other love between adult men and young boys. Advocating it on loud-mouthed Downey's program was a real horror. Chain-smoking Downey tore up Coon's literature. Someone in the equally hostile audience shouted, "What they did to Ted Bundy, I'd do the same thing to you."

But after the syndicated show had aired nationally on February 21, Coon got the last laugh. He revealed himself to be an impostor.

Coon wasn't really a member of North American Man-Boy Love Association; he didn't support the group's beliefs. The last name he had given Downey's producers was false, and he wasn't really a Harvard student. He was actually a junior computer science and engineering major at MIT as well as an aspiring actor out to test his acting abilities and, along the way, prove the unreliability of what he calls "trash TV" where anyone can tell the viewers anything at all and neither they nor maybe even the broadcasters have any way of knowing if it's legitimate.

But what to pretend to be? Deciding Satan worshipers were too ordinary, he opted for men who love boys, and researched their association at the MIT library.

Serendipitously, he met the Downey show's executive producer, Bill Boggs, at a student broadcasting conference in Providence.

"Downey is the worst of trash television, so I went up to Boggs and said, 'Have you heard of NAMBLA?' He said yes and pulled out his card. I thought 'this could be good.' So I did some more research.

"I called [Boggs] and he said, 'Send some information.' So I got some from NAMBLA and mailed it to him. In February, ratings sweeps month, I got the call that they were ready to do the show."

The Downey show producers wanted several NAMBLA members, but the fellow students Coon hatched the plot with chickened out of the upcoming TV appearance.

"To rehearse, we'd simulate the show. One of my friends played Downey and I played myself, of course. He'd shout at me and I'd shout back to see how well I could stand up in an argument.

"I felt pretty confident once I got there. I was just playing a character, so when they yelled at me, their criticisms didn't affect me. There was a feeling of power that I could just sit up there and yell back at them with immunity because I knew it wasn't really me they were yelling at."

After the broadcast, Coon announced his hoax via MIT's student paper *The Tech*. "Bill Boggs threatened me with great bodily harm and used a lot of expletives, but my lawyer doubts that they'll sue me since I'm a student—I have no money and they'd get a lot of bad publicity." He's heard nothing from NAMBLA.

So what's next? "My next step is to get on Geraldo, but I'm probably blacklisted from trash TV."

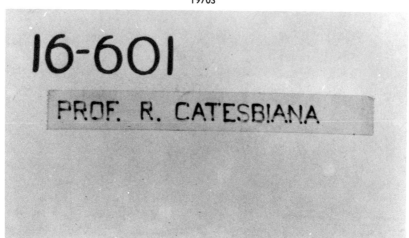

Ribbit

Professor Catesbiana was invented by students and assigned an "office" in a lab where American bullfrogs were kept for research on amphibian immune systems. The scientific name of the American bullfrog is *rana catesbiana*. Prof. Catesbiana had a penchant for writing letters to newspapers—an example is this letter printed in the *Boston Globe* in which the professor discussed the John Hancock Tower. (Owing to materials problems, the building had been losing windows and many had been boarded up with plywood.)

WOODLESS HANCOCK INDISTINCT

Upon my recent return to Boston after an absence of several years, I noticed a drastic alteration in one of Boston's most famous landmarks; I refer to the John Hancock Tower in Copley Square. While I must admit that, as it now stands, this building is quite attractive—and the "mirror effect" from the glass windows is particularly striking on a sunny day—yet I also believe that, due to the alteration in this building since I was last there, Boston has lost a good deal of its charm and singularity.

A sixty-story-tall plywood and steel building was a rarity. Pilots of planes in holding patterns over Boston would always point it out to their passengers. It was written about many times in magazines; tourists came here to marvel at it and, perhaps, watch a giant window fall. It was unique; now, alas, it is just another skyscraper.

MISCELLANEOUS PRINTED WORKS

Gadsby

Written by an alumnus of the class of 1889, this unusual 50,110 word novel was finished in 1936 and published in 1939. The book tells of John Gadsby and the Youth of Branton Hills and how they worked to transform a small stagnant agricultural town into a healthy community with a multitude of cultural, social, and technical resources. Wright's introduction to the book describes how this literary novelty was created:

The entire manuscript of this story was written with the E type-bar of the typewriter *tied down*; thus making it impossible for that letter to be printed. This was done so that none of that vowel might slip in, accidentally; and many *did* try to do so! . . .

In writing such a story,—purposely avoiding all words containing the vowel E, there are a great many difficulties. The greatest of these is met in the past tense of verbs, almost all of which end with "—ed." Therefore substitutes must be found; and they are *very few*. This will cause, at times, a somewhat monotonous use of such words as "said;" for neither "replied," "answered" nor "asked" can be used. Another difficulty comes with the elimination of the common couplet "of course," and its very common connective, "consequently;" which will, unavoidably cause "bumpy spots." The numerals also cause plenty of trouble, for none between six and thirty are available. When introducing young ladies into the story, this is a *real* barrier; for what young woman wants to have it known that she is over thirty? And this restriction on numbers, of course taboos all mention of dates.

Many abbreviations also must be avoided; the most common of all, "Mr." and "Mrs." being particularly troublesome; for those words, if read aloud, plainly indicate the E in their orthography.

As the letter E is used more than five times oftener than any other letter, this story was written, not through any attempt to attain literary merit, but due to a somewhat balky nature, caused by hearing it so constantly claimed that "it can't be done; for you *cannot* say anything at all without using E, and make a smooth continuity, with perfectly grammatical construction—" so 'twas said. . . .

Pronouns also caused trouble; for such words as he, she, they, them, theirs, her, herself, myself, himself, yourself, etc., could not be utilized. But a particularly annoying obstacle comes when, almost through a long paragraph you find no words with which to continue that line of thought; hence, as in Solitaire, you are "stuck," and must go way back and start another; which, of course, must perfectly fit the preceding context.

. . . The story required five and a half months of concentrated endeavor, with so many erasures and retrenchments that I tremble as I think of them. Of course anybody can write such a story. All that is needed is a piece of string tied from the E type-bar down to some part of the base of the typewriter. Then simply go ahead and type your story. Incidentally, you should have some sort of a bromide preparation handy, for use when the going gets rough, as it most assuredly will!

. . . I have even ordered the printer not to head each chapter with the words "Chapter 2," etc., on account of that bothersome E in that word.

Some excerpts from the story:

III

Youth cannot stay for long in a condition of inactivity; and so, for only about a month did things so stand, until a particularly bright girl in our Organization, thought out a plan for caring for infants of folks who had to go out, to work; and this bright kid soon had a group of girls who would join, during vacation, in voluntarily giving up four days a month to such work. With about fifty girls collaborating, all districts had this most gracious aid; and a girl would not only watch and guard, but would also instruct, as far as practical, any such tot as had not had its first schooling. Such Work by young girls still in school was a grand thing; and Gadsby not only stood up for such loyalty, but got at his boys to find a similar plan; and soon had a full troop of Boy Scouts; uniforms and all. This automatically brought about a Girl Scout unit; and, through a collaboration of both, a form of club sprang up. It was a club in which any boy or girl of a family owning a car would call mornings for pupils having no cars, during school days, for a trip to school and back. This was not only a saving in long walks for many, but also took from a young back, that hard, tiring strain from lugging such armfuls of books as you find pupils laboriously carrying today. Upon arriving at a school building, many cars would unload so many books that Gadsby said:—

"You would think that a Public Library branch was moving in!" This car work soon brought up a thought of giving similar aid to ailing adults; who, not owning a car, could not know of that vast display of hill and plain so common to a majority of our townsfolks. So a plan was laid, by which a car would call two days a month; and for an hour or so, follow roads winding out of town and through woods, farm lands and suburbs; showing distant ponds, and that grand arch of sky which "shut-ins" know only from photographs. Ah; *how* that plan did stir up joyous anticipation amongst such as thus had an opportunity to call upon old, loving pals, and talk of old customs and past days!

VII

Now that a zoo was actually on its way, Gadsby had to call in various groups to talk about what a Zoo should contain. Now you know that *all* animals can't find room in this orthographically odd story; so if you visit Lucy zoo, you'll miss a customary inhabitant, or two. But you'll find an array worthy of your trip. So a call was put in two big daily journals, asking for bids on animals and birds; and soon, from north, south and crisscross points, a hunting party or a city with too many zoo animals on hand got in touch with Branton Hills, with proposals for all kinds of animals, from kangaroos to bats; and our Organization had a lot of fun planning how many it could crowd into City Park, without crowding out visitors. Finally a ballot put Lucy's zoological population as follows:—

First, according to Lucy, "an awfully, AWFULLY big hippopotamus, with a pool for its comfort;" a yak, caribou, walrus, (also with a pool,) a long fox-run, bisons, gnus, stags, (it was a stag, you know, that got this zoo plan going!), alligators, mountain lions, African lions, wild cats, wild boars, llamas, gorillas, baboons, orang-outangs, mandrils; *and*, according to Gadsby's boys, a "big gang" of that amusing, tiny mimic always found accompanying hand-organs. Also an aviary, containing condors, buzzards, parrots, ibis, macaws, adjutant birds, storks, owls, quail, falcons, tiny humming birds, a sprinkling of hawks, mocking birds, swans, fancy ducks, toucans; and . . . All in all it would furnish a mighty amusing and popular spot which would draw lots of out of town visitors . . .

"A Poem"

The following poem was submitted by a student, passed the review process, and was published in the Winter-Spring 1966 issue of *Tangent,* a student-run literary magazine published from the late 1950s through the early 1970s. Unbeknownst to the editors, the author incorporated a hidden critique of the magazine in "A Poem."

Born of but malevolent intentions,
Utilizing cunning, artful means,
Laughing at excusable pretensions,
Longing for the "truth" that only "seems,"
Sneering at all virtue and achievement,
Hiding impotence behind a scornful veil,
Inside, a twisted knot of hate and torment,
The Bad Guy come a ridin' down the trail.

M.J.M '68

CAN Magazine

A 44-page literary magazine of poetry, stories, drawings, and photo collages, *Can Magazine* was distinguished by its unique wrapper—the magazine came rolled up in a can. The editor commented, "I suppose you could call the whole thing a parody of pop art." The publication proved to be troublesome for the editor; although American Can Company provided 1,000 sixteen-ounce cans for the project, the magazine was too tall for the capping machine to seal the can. Usen Canning Company then came to the rescue by allowing the editor to use a hand-operated capper to finish his creation.

Alphabetic Number Tables

This handy manual was published for April Fools' Day in 1972.

Alphabetic Number Tables

0 - 1000

18.051 NUMBERS GANG / 1972

PREFACE

It gives us great pleasure, not unmixed with profound emotion, to at last make public these alphabetical tabulations of the natural integers, ordered both in English literation and in Roman numerals.

Availing ourselves of the unmatched technological facilities of this Institute, we have developed, compiled, and revised these listings in the hope of bridging the cultural gap separating theoretical investigation and practical application.

Although the idea of such a tabulation is not new, we nevertheless trust that the appearance of this volume, meagre as it is, bespeaks the possibility of further work along similar lines.

Our humble enterprise is motivated by an honest desire to make this work an invaluable aid to the teaching profession, the mathematician, the physical scientist, the engineer, the statistician, and to many others, whose use of these pages will facilitate solution of challenging problems in all intellectual endeavours.

At MIT   AZ
Cambridge, Mass. DB
1 April 1972   GCR
                  RC
                  MP

PAGE 5

#	English	Number	Roman
1	eight	8	VIII
2	eight hundred	800	DCCC
3	eight hundred eight	808	DCCCVIII
4	eight hundred eighteen	818	DCCCXVIII
5	eight hundred eighty	880	DCCCLXXX
6	eight hundred eighty-eight	888	DCCCLXXXVIII
7	eight hundred eighty-five	885	DCCCLXXXV
8	eight hundred eighty-four	884	DCCCLXXXIV
9	eight hundred eighty-nine	889	DCCCLXXXIX
10	eight hundred eighty-one	881	DCCCLXXXI
11	eight hundred eighty-seven	887	DCCCLXXXVII
12	eight hundred eighty-six	886	DCCCLXXXVI
13	eight hundred eighty-three	883	DCCCLXXXIII
14	eight hundred eighty-two	882	DCCCLXXXII
15	eight hundred eleven	811	DCCCXI
16	eight hundred fifteen	815	DCCCXV
17	eight hundred fifty	850	DCCCL
18	eight hundred fifty-eight	858	DCCCLVIII
19	eight hundred fifty-five	855	DCCCLV
20	eight hundred fifty-four	854	DCCCLIV
21	eight hundred fifty-nine	859	DCCCLIX
22	eight hundred fifty-one	851	DCCCLI
23	eight hundred fifty-seven	857	DCCCLVII
24	eight hundred fifty-six	856	DCCCLVI
25	eight hundred fifty-three	853	DCCCLIII
26	eight hundred fifty-two	852	DCCCLII
27	eight hundred five	805	DCCCV
28	eight hundred forty	840	DCCCXL
29	eight hundred forty-eight	848	DCCCXLVIII
30	eight hundred forty-five	845	DCCCXLV
31	eight hundred forty-four	844	DCCCXLIV
32	eight hundred forty-nine	849	DCCCXLIX
33	eight hundred forty-one	841	DCCCXLI
34	eight hundred forty-seven	847	DCCCXLVII
35	eight hundred forty-six	846	DCCCXLVI
36	eight hundred forty-three	843	DCCCXLIII
37	eight hundred forty-two	842	DCCCXLII
38	eight hundred four	804	DCCCIV
39	eight hundred fourteen	814	DCCCXIV
40	eight hundred nine	809	DCCCIX
41	eight hundred nineteen	819	DCCCXIX
42	eight hundred ninety	890	DCCCXC
43	eight hundred ninety-eight	898	DCCCXCVIII
44	eight hundred ninety-five	895	DCCCXCV
45	eight hundred ninety-four	894	DCCCXCIV
46	eight hundred ninety-nine	899	DCCCXCIX
47	eight hundred ninety-one	891	DCCCXCI
48	eight hundred ninety-seven	897	DCCCXCVII
49	eight hundred ninety-six	896	DCCCXCVI
50	eight hundred ninety-three	893	DCCCXCIII

PAGE 6

#	English	Number	Roman
51	eight hundred ninety-two	892	DCCCXCII
52	eight hundred one	801	DCCCI
53	eight hundred seven	807	DCCCVII
54	eight hundred seventeen	817	DCCCXVII
55	eight hundred seventy	870	DCCCLXX
56	eight hundred seventy-eight	878	DCCCLXXVIII
57	eight hundred seventy-five	875	DCCCLXXV
58	eight hundred seventy-four	874	DCCCLXXIV
59	eight hundred seventy-nine	879	DCCCLXXIX
60	eight hundred seventy-one	871	DCCCLXXI
61	eight hundred seventy-seven	877	DCCCLXXVII
62	eight hundred seventy-six	876	DCCCLXXVI
63	eight hundred seventy-three	873	DCCCLXXIII
64	eight hundred seventy-two	872	DCCCLXXII
65	eight hundred six	806	DCCCVI
66	eight hundred sixteen	816	DCCCXVI
67	eight hundred sixty	860	DCCCLX
68	eight hundred sixty-eight	868	DCCCLXVIII
69	eight hundred sixty-five	865	DCCCLXV
70	eight hundred sixty-four	864	DCCCLXIV
71	eight hundred sixty-nine	869	DCCCLXIX
72	eight hundred sixty-one	861	DCCCLXI
73	eight hundred sixty-seven	867	DCCCLXVII
74	eight hundred sixty-six	866	DCCCLXVI
75	eight hundred sixty-three	863	DCCCLXIII
76	eight hundred sixty-two	862	DCCCLXII
77	eight hundred ten	810	DCCCX
78	eight hundred thirteen	813	DCCCXIII
79	eight hundred thirty	830	DCCCXXX
80	eight hundred thirty-eight	838	DCCCXXXVIII
81	eight hundred thirty-five	835	DCCCXXXV
82	eight hundred thirty-four	834	DCCCXXXIV
83	eight hundred thirty-nine	839	DCCCXXXIX
84	eight hundred thirty-one	831	DCCCXXXI
85	eight hundred thirty-seven	837	DCCCXXXVII
86	eight hundred thirty-six	836	DCCCXXXVI
87	eight hundred thirty-three	833	DCCCXXXIII
88	eight hundred thirty-two	832	DCCCXXXII
89	eight hundred three	803	DCCCIII
90	eight hundred twelve	812	DCCCXII
91	eight hundred twenty	820	DCCCXX
92	eight hundred twenty-eight	828	DCCCXXVIII
93	eight hundred twenty-five	825	DCCCXXV
94	eight hundred twenty-four	824	DCCCXXIV
95	eight hundred twenty-nine	829	DCCCXXIX
96	eight hundred twenty-one	821	DCCCXXI
97	eight hundred twenty-seven	827	DCCCXXVII
98	eight hundred twenty-six	826	DCCCXXVI
99	eight hundred twenty-three	823	DCCCXXIII
100	eight hundred twenty-two	822	DCCCXXII

PAGE 27

#	Roman	Number	#	Roman	Number
1	C	100	51	CCCVII	307
2	CC	200	52	CCCVIII	308
3	CCC	300	53	CCCX	310
4	CCCI	301	54	CCCXC	390
5	CCCII	302	55	CCCXCI	391
6	CCCIII	303	56	CCCXCII	392
7	CCCIV	304	57	CCCXCIII	393
8	CCCIX	309	58	CCCXCIV	394
9	CCCL	350	59	CCCXCIX	399
10	CCCLI	351	60	CCCXCV	395
11	CCCLII	352	61	CCCXCVI	396
12	CCCLIII	353	62	CCCXCVII	397
13	CCCLIV	354	63	CCCXCVIII	398
14	CCCLIX	359	64	CCCXI	311
15	CCCLV	355	65	CCCXII	312
16	CCCLVI	356	66	CCCXIII	313
17	CCCLVII	357	67	CCCXIV	314
18	CCCLVIII	358	68	CCCXIX	319
19	CCCLX	360	69	CCCXL	340
20	CCCLXI	361	70	CCCXLI	341
21	CCCLXII	362	71	CCCXLII	342
22	CCCLXIII	363	72	CCCXLIII	343
23	CCCLXIV	364	73	CCCXLIV	344
24	CCCLXIX	369	74	CCCXLIX	349
25	CCCLXV	365	75	CCCXLV	345
26	CCCLXVI	366	76	CCCXLVI	346
27	CCCLXVII	367	77	CCCXLVII	347
28	CCCLXVIII	368	78	CCCXLVIII	348
29	CCCLXX	370	79	CCCXV	315
30	CCCLXXI	371	80	CCCXVI	316
31	CCCLXXII	372	81	CCCXVII	317
32	CCCLXXIII	373	82	CCCXVIII	318
33	CCCLXXIV	374	83	CCCXX	320
34	CCCLXXIX	379	84	CCCXXI	321
35	CCCLXXV	375	85	CCCXXII	322
36	CCCLXXVI	376	86	CCCXXIII	323
37	CCCLXXVII	377	87	CCCXXIV	324
38	CCCLXXVIII	378	88	CCCXXIX	329
39	CCCLXXX	380	89	CCCXXV	325
40	CCCLXXXI	381	90	CCCXXVI	326
41	CCCLXXXII	382	91	CCCXXVII	327
42	CCCLXXXIII	383	92	CCCXXVIII	328
43	CCCLXXXIV	384	93	CCCXXX	330
44	CCCLXXXIX	389	94	CCCXXXI	331
45	CCCLXXXV	385	95	CCCXXXII	332
46	CCCLXXXVI	386	96	CCCXXXIII	333
47	CCCLXXXVII	387	97	CCCXXXIX	339
48	CCCLXXXVIII	388	98	CCCXXXIX	339
49	CCCV	305	99	CCCXXXV	335
50	CCCVI	306	100	CCCXXXVI	336

Killian Currency

CLOSE ENOUGH
FOR JAZZ

The Ugliest Homecoming Queen on Campus

Every fall since 1953, Alpha Phi Omega, the MIT service fraternity, has held the Ugliest Man on Campus charity contest. The candidate who collects the most money for charity is declared U.M.O.C. (pronounced "you-mock"). In the fall of 1978, the winner collected $1,249 for the American Cancer Society and won the grand prize which included a candlelight dinner for two at McDonald's. For MIT's first (in modern times) homecoming football game, the U.M.O.C. was declared the homecoming queen and rode on a float. Having been bestowed this honor, he entered a national competition for homecoming queens in America. Although he met all the requirements, his entry was refused.

OCTOBER 1978

Arachnoid

Constructed with 1,250 feet of nylon rope and steel wire to secure the joints, the Burton Spider Web was the result of extensive research; an electron microscope was used to determine the texture of spider webs and an arachnologist was consulted before the web was constructed.

STUDENTS TAKING "ART AND THE ENVIRONMENT" / APRIL 1976

The Baker Piano Recital

The Bruno is a unit of volume equal to the size of the dent in an asphalt surface resulting from the six-story free fall of an upright piano. The experiment was first performed on October 24, 1972 determining that the Bruno is equal to 1158 cubic centimeters. The Bruno was named after the student who suggested the experiment as a method for disposing of a worn-out piano in the dormitory. The fall was documented with audio equipment and high-speed movie cameras. Further analysis of the data indicated that the piano was traveling at 43 miles per hour and had 45,000 foot-pounds of energy at impact. In order to verify the results, this experiment was repeated every year that a suitable piano was available. In 1984, Amherst Alley was relocated thus eliminating the test site.

1978

1983

1972

1980

1975

1978

1983

Building Cozy

In 1982, Avon Books published Alfred Gingold's parody of the L. L. Bean catalog. The items listed included edible moccasins, brassieres for dogs, cheddar cheese flavored tongue depressors, and sheepskin-lined cases for canned tuna. The Real Estate Officer at MIT sent a purchase order to the publisher for a building cozy to protect the Green Building. A while later, the following correspondence ensued:

Deerskin Dieter's Mask

Discourages food intake. Completely covers face, including nose, ears, chin, throat, and mouth. Neckstrap and headstrap lock from behind, provide snug fit. Breath-through nose and mouth perforations prevent both suffocation and ingestion. Supple, full-grain deerskin stays soft and strong after repeated wetting, tugging, biting, and scraping. Removal instructions included. Neutral colors will not draw attention when worn in public.

Three colors: Normal. Ethnic. Camouflage.
AARGH Deerskin Dieter's Mask, $11.25 ppd.

Edible Moccasin

Combines walking comfort, durability, and digestibility. True moccasin construction cradles the foot. "Beef Roll" cross strap is made of dried beef, rolled and sewn in place with heavily varnished linguine filament. Filament may be used for trail snack or eaten as simple pasta course with a light cream sauce and a few turns of a pepper mill. Heel counter and hand-sewn toe piece are made of pita dough laminated to a layer of waxed, hand-rubbed beef jerky. Provides snug, foot-conforming fit and tasty open sandwich.

Stiff mid-sole is replaced in this shoe by a layer of whipped topping sewn in for added support, cushioning, and a light dessert. Rest of shoe may be used in casseroles, stews, etc.

Color: Roast Brown. Weight about 2 lbs.
Men's sizes: 8-13, (No size 12-1/2.)
Three widths: B, D, and E.
Size 10D serves two. No substitutions.
561CW Men's Edible Moccasin, $41.75 ppd.

Building Cozy

Insulated Building Cozy provides heat retention and abrasion resistance for large urban structures. Heavy duty, pre-shrunk gingham is treated for water repellency. Bright colors will not fade for life of cozy. First-quality bunting insulation protects from high winds, sleet and blimps travelling up to 30 knots. Taffeta lining will not snag corners, window frames or trim.

Wide, "easy-alter" hem can be let in or out with ease. Weight about 50¼ tons. Machine Washable. Stuff sack included.
Three colors: Red Check. Blue Check. Camouflage.
Three sizes: Seagram, Empire, World Trade.
6RMS RIVVW   Building Cozy, $51,575.25 ppd.

December 17, 1982

Gentlemen:

A month ago we forwarded to you our purchase order #ES437192 for a Building Cozy for our Earth Sciences Building; color - red check.

We have not received confirmation of our order; however, if the shipment is in the mail (or possibly on a Conrail car), we will forward our check in the amount of $51,575.25 as soon as the order is received.

Thank you for attention to this matter, and we wish you Best Wishes for a successful Holiday Season!

Sincerely,

Philip A. Trussell

January 10, 1983

Dear Mister Trussell:

We are in receipt of your order for Item #6RMS RIVVW, Building Cozy, Red Check Model. Unfortunately, we have just received a similar order from the Port Authority of New York and New Jersey. Since this will undoubtedly consume the entire supply of good, honest American red-checked gingham that we might possibly import from Hong Kong over the next few years—to say nothing of the entire East Coast supply of seamstresses and seamsters—I am afraid that we will not be able to guarantee delivery of your order before the next ice age cometh.

In the meantime, perhaps you should consider individual orders of the Solar Watch Cap, which is sturdy enough to warm the most professorial brain.

Yours sincerely,

Ann C. McKeown
Publicity Manager

On January 20, 1983, a flatbed truck with a large crate arrived at MIT surprising *almost* everyone in the office. The Real Estate Officer was called down to sign for the building cozy.

The Primrose Path

The "nerd path" across Kresge Oval was created by students taking short-cuts across the grass. One morning, pedestrians found that the 122-foot path had been planted overnight with pink, purple, lavender, white, lilac, and crimson primroses. As a final touch, the ends of the path were planted with a different flower—impatiens.

CHINA ALTMAN (WITH SUPPORT FROM THE COUNCIL FOR THE ARTS AT MIT AND ASSISTANCE FROM ATO) / MAY 1984

VOO DOO

Voo Doo was the campus humor magazine from 1919 through 1976. From the 1940s through the sixties, *Voo Doo* often staged elaborate publicity stunts to publicize new issues.

Voo Doo staged a reenactment of the Civil War battle of the *Merrimac* and the *Monitor* on the Charles River.

SPRING 1955

In October of 1947, *Voo Doo* held a ground-breaking ceremony taking credit for the construction of a new dormitory. The next day, MIT president Karl Taylor Compton held the official groundbreaking.

OCTOBER 1947

For their "Pseudo Scientific American" issue, the *Voo Doo* staff set up a "time machine" to bring back the first Boston city planner. The machine produced a calf. (According to Boston folklore, the city streets began as cow paths.)

DECEMBER 1958

For MIT Open House, *Voo Doo* built a 12-foot-long Dipsy Duck hooked to a generator that supposedly produced 3.14159 volts. *Voo Doo* claimed that 250-foot-long Dipsy Ducks could be built next to rivers to produce electricity. It also reported that the Duck worked slower when powered with beer. Careful inspection revealed that a motor was powering the Dipsy Duck.

APRIL 1948

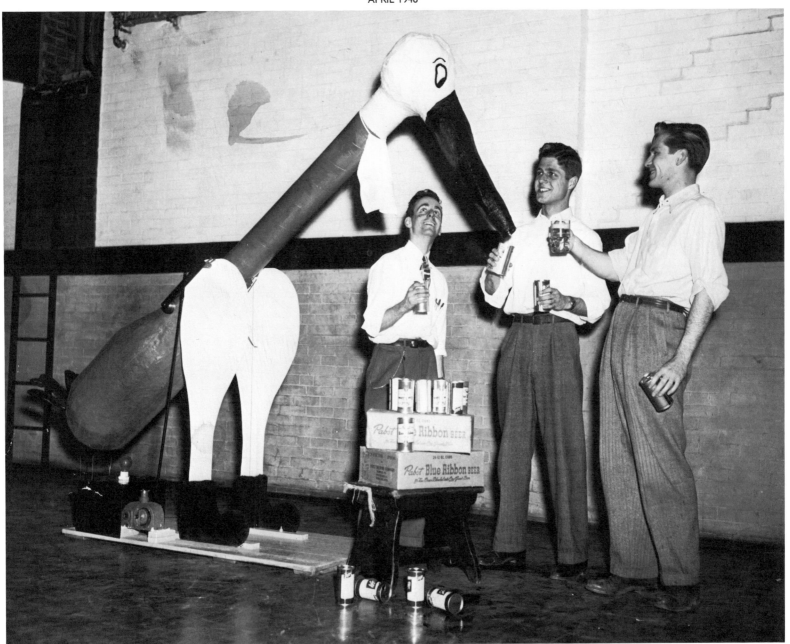

VOO DOO

In the summer of 1965, the *Voo Doo* staff chose five hundred incoming freshmen at random and invited them to join the honor society Sigma Alpha Pi. Each freshman was asked to fill out a questionnaire and to submit a photo. A total of 343 responses were received. Only fifteen of them saw through the hoax and replied appropriately. Excerpts from the replies were printed in *Voo Doo*. The pictures sent in by SAP freshmen were displayed at the *Voo Doo* sales table; freshmen who bought a copy of *Voo Doo* were allowed to remove their picture.

OCTOBER 1965

VOO DOO
BRIDGE

IN MEMORIAM TO THE CURLEY GRAFT GEN-
ERATOR, HITHERTO THE MOST SUCCESSFUL
PERPETUAL MOTION MACHINE KNOWN.
AND IN RECOGNITION OF THE HYNES SIGHT
AND WISDOM RESPONSIBLE FOR ITS DEMISE.

VOO DOO

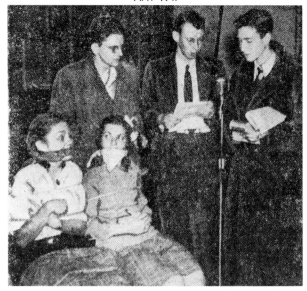

Inspired by Orson Welles' "War of the Worlds" radio show, *Voo Doo* arranged a hoax at the Wellesley College radio station. A Beethoven piano sonata was interrupted with the sounds of a struggle between the radio station staff and invaders. The leader of the intruders announced plans to "set up an electromorphic flux and contrapolar micro-reflector with which to create neutral mesons to blow up the college!"

At the end came a commercial: "The preceding program has been presented through the courtesy of *Voo Doo,* the monthly humor magazine of MIT. *Voo Doo* will be on sale tomorrow . . . at 25 cents per copy. Don't forget. Buy *Voo Doo!*" Afterward, the Wellesley women posed with the invaders for press photographers.

Stunt features 'copter

Voo Doo goes "ape" in Great Court

By Tom Rozsa

Voo Doo soared to new heights on Friday as several copies of the slightly gross publication were carried aloft in a helicopter by a half-crazed gorilla.

Voo Doo's first publication for the new school year went on sale Friday, October 15. Traditionally, the staff of Tech's wildest publication plans a publicity stunt to give students an indication as to what they might discover if they read Voo Doo.

Faunch championship planned

At 12 p.m., Voo Doo held the first annual American Faunch championship, to be played on the Great Court. Faunch is a jolly game which was first played by the ancient Aztec Indians and was later discovered by the Spaniards. Apparently the game did not win universal acclaim for no one since the conquistadors has played it. That is, not until a VD staff member discovered this exciting sport in an old volume in the Humanities Library.

Walt Kuleck, '67, Makeup Editor of Voo Doo was the announcer and referee of the contest. As he began to announce the rules of the game of faunch, a large crowd of Techmen and visitors to the Institute gathered around him. He emphasized the fact that it was Virgil's birthday and therefore the winner of the contest would receive a sixpack of Virgil's birthday cheer.

The game is similar to soccer; however in faunch, the contest is held with humans acting as goal posts. The faunch balls used by the ancient Aztecs were made of cow intestines, however, due to a shortage of cows around MIT, Walt used two square cardboard boxes as substitutes for faunch balls. The faunch playing field consisted of half of the Great

Photo by John Torode
Voo Doo helicopter seen landing in the middle of the Faunch field laid out in the Great Court.

Court. The area was roped off and several campus policemen were on hand for the festivities.

Guzzlers challenge tools

The faunch team consists of three players. The Voo Doo team, named the Guzzlers, consisted of John Marshall, playing left gronk; Dave Ellis, at rught fuch; and Bob Pyndyck backing up as center shuvenuoors. Walt asked for three volunteers to play against this murderous team and surprisingly enough three techmen volunteered. The contest was ready to begin with the exception of one major drawback — referee Walt Kulck was having a difficult time trying to get volunteers to act as goal posts.

In the midst of the slight confusion, someone suddenly yelled out: "Look, up in the sky," a helicopter, and it was landing right in the middle of the faunch playing field.

This slightly upset the impending contest. It looked as though the game would be over before it got started, however, the action was just beginning. Out of the helicopter jumped a gorilla, played by Mike Levine, General Manager of Voo Doo. Apparently the gorilla was extremely interested in purchasing several copies of Voo Doo for he ran directly to right fuch, Dave Ellis, who was selling pre-game issues of Voo Doo.

Apparently the gorilla did not know that the price of Voo Doo had increased from 35c. to 40c. a copy. The right fuch demanded 40c. and the gorilla promptly refused. After a considerable argument, the gorilla grabbed a copy of the emerald colored issue and threw 35c. at the right fuch.

Upset gorilla upsets Doo Doo

Suddenly a wild melee began. Dave Ellis, the right fuch attempted to regain possession of the stolen Voo Doo but the gorilla clobbered him with the issue, ripped part of the Voo Doo sign, and began to run toward the helicopter. Walt Kuleck, with some help from the left gronk, the center shuvenupors, and a slightly limping right fuch attemped to stop the gorilla while demanding the extra nickel. The gorilla, by now extremely savage, still retained part of the wooden support of the sign he had ripped, and he promptly clobbered Walt and company.

The gorilla eventually staggered to the helicopter and took off, and much to the regret of all, the game had to be called off.

After long deliberation, the VD members decided to give the game of faunch back to the Aztecs.

William Barton Rogers helps sell *Voo Doo*.

AFTERWORD

This book chronicles only a small portion of the hacks that have occurred at MIT. Hundreds of hacks are documented in the files of the MIT Museum. Many were not included in this book because insufficient material was available to present them properly. Other hacks are undocumented and exist only as part of the MIT folklore.

Whenever hacking is discussed, for example, the trolley car caper is mentioned. According to legend, students welded the wheels of a trolley to the tracks. I have heard more than a hundred accounts of this story and the details vary greatly. Most of the stories say that the event occurred in front of MIT, but some say that it occurred in Boston. Additionally, most stories say that thermite welding was used, but some say that it was done electrically using the trolley's overhead power cable. The greatest problem in documenting this hack has been uncertainty about the date that it occurred—different accounts of the event place the date anywhere from 1916 through the late 1950s.

The search for documentation of hacks, old and new, continues—there will undoubtedly be a second edition. I welcome any contributions relating to hacks. Please send personal recollections, photos, clippings, artifacts, and possible leads to the Curator of the Institute for Hacks, TomFoolery, and Pranks at MIT, c/o MIT Museum, 265 Massachusetts Avenue, Cambridge, MA 02139.

BL

THANKS TO:

Thomas H. Adams, Dorothy Adler, Richard Adler, Gary Agrant, Dante Alighieri, Matthew Alschuler, China Altman, Alfred Anderson, Cathy Anderson, Jim Anderson, Jeff Applebaum, Anne Armitage, John Arrison, Edward Averett, Avon Books, Robert Baldwin, Charles Ball, Tom Barta, Loren Batchman, Michel B. Baylocq, Carl Bazil, Ronald E. Becker, Sally Beddow, Joan Bein, Diana ben-Aaron, Brian Bentz, Stephen P. Berczuk, Mike Bernard, Michael Bertin, Bettmann Newsphotos, Jeff Bigler, Bob Blake, Mark Bolotin, Walter Booth, John O. Borland, *The Boston Globe, The Boston Herald,* Mary Bourquin, V. Michael Bove, Morton C. Bradley, Jr., Gene Brammer, Claude Brenner, Charles Bright, Jerry Broda, Bob Brooks, Andrew Browder, Dwight Brown, Jeff Brown, Ken Browning, Bruner-Cott, Charles Bruno, Dan Bullock, Stephen Burns, Vannevar Bush, Peter Büttner, Cambridge Historical Commission, Calvin Campbell, Ken Campbell, S. Harrison Carter, Rana Catesbiana, Terrill Chang, Kenneth Chestnut, Jr., Chip, *The Christian Science Monitor,* Edward Clark, Jim Coleman, Joseph Collins, Karl Taylor Compton, Liz Connors, Marcia Conroy, John Cook, Chris Coon, Tom Coppeto, Donna Coveney, James M. Crafts, John Cronin, Chris Crowley, Susan Crowley, Linda Custer, George Dadakis, Donald Davidoff, Lee Davison, D. deAngeli, Peter deFlorez, André DeHon, Joe Dennehy, Daniel Dern, John Deutch, Larry Deutsch, Alan Devoe, William Dickson, Bob Di Iorio, Gene Dixon, Dorm Goblin, Bill Doyle, D. J. Dudzik, Micky DuPree, W. Mills Dyer, Jr., Harold Edgerton, Eleanor Egan, William Elmer, Brian Fabes, Fang, Richard Feynman, Jack E. Florey, Francesco Floris, Michel Floyd, Pat Flynn, Margo Foote, David Ford, Stan Forman, Les Frederick, John Freeman, Anthony French, Ann Friedlaender, Zalman Gaibel, Simson Garfinkel, Towash Gibbs, Ken Gifford, Alfred Gingold, Frank Giuffrida, Irene Giuffrida, Anne Glavin, Marc Goodman, Paul Gray, Dave Greenberg, Morton Grosser, Marvin Grossman, Conrad Grundlehner, Bernie Gunther, Phoebe Hackett, Gordon Haff, Paul Hanks, Carol Hanna, Ellen Harris, *Harvard Crimson,* John Harvard, Donald Hatfield, Steve Hazlerig, William Hecht, Beth Hedberg, Kjrsten Henriksen, Tom Hilton, Henry Hirsch, Henry Holtzman, C. Hongsberg, John Hopper, Paul Hsu, Rolf Huber, Fred Hutchison, Steve Immerman, Mark James, Howard W. Johnson, Vernice Jones, Linda Julien, Adam Kane, Henry B. Kane, Mark Kantrowitz, Sue Kayton, Frank Kelly, Susan Kendall, Dan Kersten, Joe Kesselman, Phil Keston, S. Jay Keyser, James R. Killian, Tom Klimowitz, Alan Kotok, Ellen Kranzer, Carl A. LaCombe, Craig Lambert, William Lane, Chun Lim Lau, Leif LaWhite, Alan Lazurus, Betty Lehrman, Arthur Leibowitz, John Lepingwell, Paula M. Lerner, Jerry Lettvin, Joan LeValle, Oren Levine, Susan Lewis, Faustino Lichauco, Philip Lieberman, Barbara Linden, Sandra Lipnoski, Greg Lobdell, John Lobdell, Gustavo Lobo, Jr., Karin Lohman, Kathryn Lombardi, Nancy Lombardi, Joan Loria, The Lounger, Richard C. Maclaurin, Margaret Mac Vicar, Carl Mann, Loretta Mannix, Morry Markovitz, Kathleen Marquis, John Mattill, Joseph Mazur, Kay McClain, Jeanne McDermott, John McGrew, Ann McKeown, Kenneth Meltsner, Gjon Mili, Charles Miller, Joanne Miller, Rich Miller, Jeff Mogul, Jonathan Montgomery, Jim Moody, John Moore, Conor Moran, Doreen Morris, Mary Morrissey, Emmett Murphy, Shava Nerad, Tien Nguyen, Ernest F. Nichols, Northeast Color Research, Sonya Nyman, Dan O'Day, James Olivieri, Joel Orlen, Kevin Osborn, Albert K. Paone, Warren Patriquin, Ezra Peisach, Douglas Pfeiffer, The Phantom, John Pitrelli, Marty Plys, Edgar Allan Poe, Marc PoKempner, Mary Poulos, Powell, Henry S. Pritchett, J. Arthur Random, Frank Revi, Barbara Rich, Harper V. Richards, Al Ritter, Mark Rockoff, Barry Roderick, William Barton Rogers, Cornelius Roosevelt, Robert Rose, Louis Rosenblum, Tom Rozsa, John D. Runkle, Tom Russ, Kenneth Russell, John Salozzo, Helen Samuels, George Sanborn, Heidi Saraceno, David Saxon, E. Robert Schildkraut, Jonathan Schlefer, Frank Schoettler, Tony Scivetti, Warren Seamans, Stacy Segal, Kenneth Segel, Janet Serman, Donald Severance, Elisabeth Shaw, Robert Shaw, Richard Shea, Harvey Shew, Constantine B. Simonides, Steve Slesinger, Frank L. Smith, Oliver Reed Smoot, Jr., Donald Stidsen, Steven Stoller, Julius A. Stratton, Samuel W. Stratton, Glenn Strehle, Bruce Sylvester, *The Tab, The Tech, Technique, Technology Review, Tech Talk,* Stephen Teicher, Karen Tenney, James E. Tetazoo, Kevin Theobald, Jeff Thiemann, Kathleen Thurston, Jenifer Tidwell, TMRC, John Torode, Philip Trussell, Marj Tyler, Sandy Ung, Omar S. Valerio, Paula Van Lare, Mark Vershel, Charles Vest, Mark Virtue, *Voo Doo,* Kenneth Wadleigh, Francis A. Walker, Jean Warren, Adolph Warsher, David M. Watson, Robert Weatherall, Donna Webber, William Wegerer, Rebecca Weiss, Don Whiston, Douglas White, Elizabeth Whittaker, Jerome Wiesner, Jon Williams, Sarah Wineman, Frank Winsor, Paul Winsor, August Witt, Ernest Wright, Beverly Yates, Plerbs Ydlebops, Michael Yeates, Ted Young, and many others.

PHOTO CREDITS

Where the photographer is unknown, the credit is omitted.

47	bottom, Jeff Thiemann.	98	Ellen Kranzer.
48	Ellen Kranzer.	99	top, Mike Bernard (Technique).
49	Tom Russ (Technique).		bottom, Ellen Kranzer.
50	Oren Levine (Technique).	100	all, Bob Brooks.
53	Calvin Campbell (Tech Talk).	102	left, Brian Leibowitz.
56	top and bottom, (Technique).		right, drawn by Dick Deke.
57	top center, Dan O'Day	103	(Boston Globe).
	(Technique).	104	cartoon by Bezark.
	top and bottom right, Paul	107	top and bottom, C. Hongsberg
	Winsor.		(The Tech).
61	Stephen Teicher (The Tech).	109	Brian Leibowitz.
62	left, (Technique).	110	(The Tech).
	top and bottom right,	111	(The Tech).
	(Technique).	112	Gordon Haff.
63	top left, Conrad Grundlehner	113	Brian Leibowitz.
	(The Tech).	114	Brian Leibowitz.
	bottom left, (Technique).	126	Brian Leibowitz.
	center, Leif LaWhite	130	Frank Kelly.
	(Technique).	131	Margo Foote (Tech Talk).
	top and bottom right,	132	drawn by Donald Hatfield.
	(Technique).	134	top and bottom, Gordon Haff.
	middle right, (Voo Doo).	135	Calvin Campbell (Tech Talk).
64	Fred Hutchison.	136	left, Al Ritter (Technique).
65	top, Joe Dennehy (Boston		center, Donald Davidoff
	Globe).		(Technique).
	bottom, Ronald E. Becker (The		right, Harold Edgerton.
	Tech).	137	upper middle, Carl Mann
65	Frank Schoettler.		(Technique).
66	Frank Schoettler.		lower middle, Harold Edgerton.
68	top, (Technique).		bottom, Donald Davidoff
	bottom, Stephen P. Berczuk		(Technique).
	(The Tech).	140	Albert K. Paone.
70	Mark James.	141	right, Calvin Campbell (Tech
71	right, (Technique).		Talk).
73	UPI/Bettmann Newsphotos.		top, Paul Hsu (The Tech).
74	right and left, (Technique).		bottom, (The Tech).
76	Tom Coppeto (The Tech).	143	rightmost graphic, Henry B.
77	Michel B. Baylocq (Technique).		Kane.
78	Brian Leibowitz.		upper left graphic, William
81	Brian Leibowitz.		Elmer.
85	Brian Leibowitz.		lower left graphic, Harper V.
87	Brian Leibowitz.		Richards.
88	top, Tom Barta.		bottom, R. K.
	bottom left, Simson Garfinkel	144	top, (Technique).
	(The Tech).		bottom, A Philip Lieberman.
	bottom right, Kevin Osborn	145	top, (The Tech).
	(The Tech).	146	Warren Patriguin (The Boston
89	top, John Lepingwell		Herald).
	(Technique).	147	(Technique).
92	Gene Dixon (Boston Herald	148	(The Tech).
	American).	149	bottom, (The Boston Herald).
93	(Technique).	150	John Torode (The Tech).
94	(Boston Globe).	151	Gjon Mili.
95	left, (The Tech).		
	right, Powell (The Tech).		Back Cover, Jane Reed (Harvard
96	Linda Custer (The Tech).		Magazine).

PHOTO CREDITS